An Interpretation of African
Parapsychology and Synchronicity

An Interpretation of African Parapsychology and Synchronicity

by

M. Chinkwita

The Pentland Press Limited
Edinburgh • Cambridge • Durham • USA

© M. Chinkwita 1997

First published in 1997 by
The Pentland Press Ltd.
1 Hutton Close
South Church
Bishop Auckland
Durham

British Library Cataloguing in Publication Data.
A Catalogue record for this book is available
from the British Library.

ISBN 1 85821 528 5

Typeset by George Wishart & Associates, Whitley Bay.
Printed and bound by Antony Rowe Ltd., Chippenham.

To Sr. Alma K Binder,
former missionary in Malawi
who helped me with my school fees
and to my brother Stensfield Chinkwita.

Acknowledgements

I would like to thank all the contributors to this publication. My particular thanks go to Professor Bradshaw, who patiently checked the manuscript in its final form, and also to Miss Pat Bryden of Edinburgh, a former teacher in Malawi, for assisting me to find someone to write the foreword; to Dr Vince Arkley for his constructive suggestions, comments and contribution on seriality coincidences. Thanks also to John Jalwang for introducing me to Dr Vince Arkley.

Dr A.S. Ross of Edinburgh University, Faculty of Divinity, for writing a foreword for this book.

Angela Glanville, Pauline Gorton for reading the original draft of the manuscript.

Professor Morris, Chair of Parapsychology at Edinburgh University, Department of Parapsychology, for forwarding a list of books on Parapsychology. Lena Nielson for providing me with books on coincidences.

Angus Chukuemeka, former Chair of Merseyside Racial Equality Council and Merseyside African Council, and Dr Lyson Chitsuku, for clarifying some of the points on African tradition on both seriality and synchronicity coincidences.

Rev. Willie Morris, my church Minister, Phil Purvis, my line manager, Joyce Msiska, Pat Jenkins, Sandra Edwards, Nargis Anwar, Grace Jalwang, Sandra Ledsham, Ros Burton and Jean Sanders for their opinions on this subject

Evelyn Jones, former missionary to Malawi, Dorothy Fellows, Brian Ragbourn, Margaret Liz Kewley, Carol Hannah, Mrs Margaret Chikhadzula, Mrs Violet Mtegha, Mrs Ann Andrews

(Kachingwe) Barbara King, Carol Parr and Dr and Mrs Deliah Lizi for their encouragement and support.

It would, however, be a great oversight if I did not mention my two brothers, Stensfield and Oliver Chinkwita, for their sustained encouragement. Also my niece Ellen Chinkwita for the preparation of meals while the book was in process.

Preface

I am delighted to write a preface to this book by Mary Chinkwita. As she, a Malawian, has made a second home in Britain, so I, a Scot, think of Malawi as my other home. In a brilliant recent book, *On Encountering the West*, Lamin Sanneh, Professor of World Christianity at Yale, has presented an intellectual challenge to the arrogant presumption that the western experience of life is the definitive experience for all humanity. This thoughtful book by Mary Chinkwita, the result of wide-ranging reading in post-Enlightenment scientific and psychological literature as well as of her own experience as an African woman, is another contribution to this cultural debate. This debate is an important one, for so much of the western academic world is far too insulated from the thought-world of the majority of the human beings on earth who live in Africa, Asia and Latin America. In particular, the world of formal Christian theology is particularly cut off from that thought world, this despite the fact that Christians of North America and Europe are now distinctly outnumbered by the Christians of Africa and Asia alone, without the addition of those from Latin America. As a result, so much of Christian theological writing and Biblical interpretation is done with no regard to the world view of the majority of Christians. The world of dreams is ignored in western theological writing, yet, for example, most African Christian clergy, both Catholic and Protestant, have come to their calling through the agency of dreams. It is her African version of the non-western world view that Mary Chinkwita so effectively displays in this book in an interesting interaction with modern post-Enlightenment thought. It is a serious contribution to a debate that Christian thought in particular must start to take seriously.

Andrew C. Ross
Edinburgh University

Contents

Introduction

This book mainly discusses coincidences of different kinds. The title would have been 'Coincidence' but I decided on 'Synchronicity' because of my own experience. Through extensive research and the traditional value which I place on the topic, the book explores established opinions such as those of Carl Jung, the famous psychologist. I support his theory and similar ones by other experts, that synchronistic happenings are sent by God and controlled by guardian angels.

In my first book, *The Usefulness of Dreams*, I stated that dreams which occur in sleep laboratories are somehow induced and are therefore artificial. By the same token, I am advocating in this present book that the investigation of coincidences should not be related to playing cards or gambling because these are artificial situations. I believe that dreams as well as coincidences come at a specific time when God wants them to happen, in order to tell us of the future and the present. It is for this reason that the author disagreed with the records of coincidences which took place at Duke University. True coincidences are those which tend to puzzle one with the question: "Why did this happen?" In Africa, if something unusual happens, the elderly will be busy trying to analyse the event and find a reason for it.

There were problems relating to the coincidences which took place at the Duke University laboratories; some players, it was said, already knew the card sequence by surreptitiously peeping to see how the cards were arranged. I therefore contend that such coincidences are not natural, but artificial. In these circumstances I support Carl Jung's theory that there are some

1

coincidences which are meaningless and some which are meaningful.

This book will be useful to other people who share the traditional values of the author because it has cultural values and perspectives which will be of interest to them. It will also interest most authors who are non-Africans but who have written books on this topic. These authors have used scientific analysis to research this topic and have sought answers to mystifying events which fascinate people, and who may be eager to know more about it. For this reason, the book will appeal to lay people and experts alike, such as psychologists, philosophers, theologians and academics who can appreciate much of the foundation on which my work is based and would want to know more about African beliefs, which they may compare with existing literature.

The book has been written as a result of my own experiences of synchronicity, seriality and premonition, including my own dreams concerning my mother's psychic vision of her own death. I have always recorded my own coincidences and am convinced they are sent by God to help me overcome problems. I have found synchronistic coincidences, in particular, very meaningful. Meaningful coincidences have shaped my life and have shown me my destiny. I have included dreams in the same category as coincidences, as I have always sought the meaning of dreams and coincidences.

To provide a clear picture of the topic, the book has been divided into seven chapters, starting with my own mother's psychic behaviour. This chapter deals with my mother's own prediction of her death, and my own dreams concerning her death, which I have recorded as psychic forces or coincidences. I had two dreams about her which were precognitive. This chapter also discusses the psychic influences experienced by my colleague's mother, Mrs Nargis Anwar.

The second chapter deals with definitions, clarifying the terminologies.

The third chapter deals with the founders of the subject, those who first proposed the theory of coincidence, be it synchronicity or seriality.

The fourth chapter deals with seriality, which was of great interest to Paul Kammerer, an Austrian biologist. These kinds of coincidences are what Carl Jung called meaningless, but to Kammerer they meant something. I discuss some drawn from my own experience and also those of Dr. Vince Arkley.

The fifth chapter deals with synchronicity. I have discussed my own experiences and have incorporated the work of famous writers about synchronicity such as Brian Inglis, Arthur Koestler and, of course, Carl Jung himself, the discoverer of synchronicity. I have used existing literature to back up my own experiences in extra-sensory-perception.

The sixth chapter discusses the subject of telepathy, which is also one of my areas of interest. Telepathy is another element of spontaneous extra-sensory-perception, and in most cases goes together with clairvoyance. To this end, clairvoyance is also discussed here. I have again used my own experience and the existing literature regarding telepathy and clairvoyance by Alister Hardy, M. Ullman, and other writers. I discuss telepathy and clairvoyance because of their relationship with coincidence.

The seventh chapter deals with dreams concerning the future and the present. The dreams discussed here are also seen as a kind of coincidence. It also deals with words which in the end become true, yet at the time were being said for the sake of saying them. To some extent these words can be regarded as hidden truths.

Then lastly there is a conclusion in which I sum up my view and my beliefs.

CHAPTER 1

Dreams of My Mother's Death and Her Psychic Experience

Carl Jung suggested that we probably dream all the time both when we are awake (consciousness) and when we are asleep (unconsciousness), and this is a notion with which I tend to agree. I have associated it with psychic phenomena. Jung was, however, more inclined to draw a parallel between the two types of dreaming. He called those which happen while awake 'visions' or 'hallucination' and the rest 'dreams'.

I believe we all possess powers or have the gift of extra-sensory-perception; only some fail to recognise this extra, sixth sense. Psychic power is scientifically known as psychometry, which Webster, as Peter Hurkos puts it, defined as "divination of a fact concerning an object or its owner through contact with or proximity to the object".[1] Psychic experience is based on simultaneous occurrences. For example, two things may happen at the same time. One of them, as Carl Jung puts it, is the normal probable state (i.e. the one that is casually explicable), and the other, the critical experience, is the one that cannot be derived casually from the first. Psychical experience is perceived by many as 'coincidence' or 'chance'.

Psychic powers truly originate from God. It makes me sad that some churches have regarded extra-sensory-perception as mere heresy, and that some psychologists have regarded it as pathological. Yet to my mind, if it were heresy, it would not have existed up to now; it would have ceased to exist. That it continues gives me every reason to believe that God alone has ordained it. Equally, if it were pathological, as some psychologists have maintained, it would not have the power of predicting the future, let alone of guiding people.

Records of allegedly psychic happenings go back to the very dawn of civilisation, as Michael Perry observed. The religious literature of Judaism and early Christianity is full of accounts of the paranormal. The established churches, however, have been loath to have much to do with the practising of psychic powers. Many people have been interested, such as wise women and healers, but they worked apart from the church. As Perry observed, "There is much confusion in the records and much ignorance generally, in particular the confusing of mediumship with witchcraft, which was something of quite a different order."[2] Some people associated psychic phenomena with the work of the devil.

Those who had the reputation of possessing paranormal gifts, whether they were wise women, astrologers or healers, were regularly consulted by individuals from all levels of society, from the peasantry to royalty. Because of some doubts which were entertained in the nineteenth century, and the fact that this century was "also the great age of science, when the mysteries of the universe were to be unlocked by all who could examine them with patient care through the scientific method", "a group of scholars at Cambridge University decided that the time had come to set up a learned society to examine those faculties of man, real or supposed, that appeared inexplicable to science."[3] As a result, the Society for Psychical Research (SPR) was founded in 1882, with Henry Sidwick (1838-1900), Professor of Moral Philosophy at Cambridge, as its first president.

Psychic Power as a Fact or Supernatural Phenomenon

Since the SPR was founded, much research has been done both by individuals and by universities. Psychic capabilities, as B. Inglis puts it in his book *The Paranormal,* "were sometimes called 'apparitions' and 'hauntings' and the various physical phenomena called 'Spiritualistic'."[4] The SPR accepted psychic phenomena as supernatural. Some people, like Alfred Russell Wallace, objected to the term 'supernatural'. Wallace preferred to call psychic experience a fact rather than supernatural, on the grounds that "The psychic phenomena he had himself observed were facts, and as they did not accord with the established scientific canons, then the scientific canons must be revised," just as the established view of the creation had to be revised following his and Darwin's presentation of their theory of evolution.[5]

In France, Charles Richet, a physiologist, also preferred the word 'facts'. According to him, these psychic facts did not contradict any accepted scientific truths: "they are new, they are unusual, they are difficult to classify, but they do not demolish anything of what has been laboriously built up in our classic edifice."[6] In my view, psychic phenomena existed before the time of Richet although they are truly unusual. They are new only to the extent that each of them tends to puzzle each generation. They are exceptionally significant, although they were generally ignored before J.B. Rhine investigated them in the 1930s, and only then did people start respecting the field of parapsychology. Charles Richet, however, added that "People who denied their existence on a priori, 'against the laws of nature' grounds, were simply unable to distinguish between the unusual and the contradictory."[7]

However, Wallace, Crookes, Lodge and others came to accept spiritualism. Science, they maintained, "would have to accept the reality of spirit forces and the process of incorporating them into the framework would require more than minor adjustments."[8] Equally, Richet, Baron Schrenck-Notzing and those who shared the same view argued that "There was nothing wrong with orthodox materialist doctrine; it was simply being too narrowly and arbitrarily defined by scientists who continued to reject the evidence for what Richet called the 'unrecognised latent powers in the human organism'."[9] I believe these powers do manifest in us, but we do not recognise them.

A new word therefore was needed for the new science which expresses the two views above. 'Psychic experience' was accepted as useful. Myers (an inspector of schools) proposed 'supernatural'. Charles Richet (Professor of physiology in the University of Paris), suggested 'metapsychic', the counterpart of metaphysics. Richet's proposal was accepted in 1923 at the International Congress. This later proved unacceptable. Emily Boirac had suggested before the International Congress the word 'parapsychology', but Richet had objected to it on the grounds that it carried a connotation of 'erroneous psychology'.

In Germany, Max Dessoir described it as 'parapsychology'. Two of the lines of research which the SPR committees had started produced good work. However, the research work was checked carefully by Gurney, who devoted his energies to psychical research, and maintained the view that feelings, sounds were experienced only by feeble-minded or mentally deranged people.

As a consequence, the Boston medium, Leonora Piper, as well as William Jones were tested. As Brian Inglis puts it, they "established beyond reasonable doubt that she was picking up information by extra-sensory means – though whether it came from the spirit world, or from some telepathic ability of a kind never before disclosed under test conditions, remained in dispute."[10]

The President of the Society for Psychical Research, Henry Sidwick, and his wife Eleanor, however, did not believe that spirits, if they ever existed, would present themselves in such uncouth and vulgar forms. One of the most familiar encounters of the spirit 'control', John King, claimed to have been a pirate in his life on earth. "They suspected that the evidence for telekinesis had been based on deception of the kind which the Italian medium, Eusapia Palladino, had been known to practice whenever she could, levitating tables with her feet."[11]

However, it was with the publication in Boston of J. B. Rhine's monograph *Extra-Sensory-Perception*, in 1934, which described research at Duke University undertaken by students who were not aware of being possessed by psychic powers, that the public became aware of parapsychology and the academics began to take notice. Since then 'parapsychology' and 'psychical research', as Brian Inglis puts it, "have been running in tandem, the emphasis being on laboratory-type trials."[12] But other cases raise the question of why so many people believe deeply in phenomena that do not exist. D. Marks et al. conducted a brief study of natural biases and errors in human perception and suggested that "The entire spectrum of psychism, occultism and pseudoscience are products of these illusions."[13] This is why there was a conflict between the believer and the sceptic. I have a feeling this conflict will continue to exist.

It is interesting to note that there had been a number of Christians in this field, such as Perry, who maintains that "ESP is a natural phenomena of the human psyche which can be used for the glory of God."[14] It can also be recorded as "the enrichment of human life when it is understood and placed in the service of divine love, the love expressed in and through Jesus Christ."[15] It was to this end that the General Assembly of the Presbyterian Church of Scotland appointed a committee in 1922 to explore this area. It expressed the hope that those Christians "who had been vouchsafed special psychic manifestations should be encouraged to share in the life of the Church rather than to withdraw themselves from its communication."[16] The people I mentioned earlier, such as Sir William Barrett, Lord Rayleigh, Henry Sidwick and William Crookes, were themselves from religious backgrounds, and were very much disturbed by the implications of the Newtonian 'Clockwork Universe.'

It was alleged that this movement was undermining the religious faith and morality, and according to Alfred Douglas,

William Barrett wrote, in an attempt to defend psychical research, that "The paramount importance of psychical research lies in its demonstration of the fact that the physical plane is not the whole of nature, our outer conscious self the whole of our human personality. It reveals that within us all are high capacious powers, now subject to the temporary limitations imposed by our bodies; that our mind can act independently of the material brain, and therefore in all probability can survive it; that there is a Spiritual world wherein active life and intelligence exist; and it affords slowly accumulating scientific proof that our life here is not a 'paltry misery closed in the grave', but the introduction to a larger life and infinite hope. Immersed in sense and outward things, the soul in many has lost its wings, but the phenomena we have been considering irradiate "the great world's altar-stairs that slope through darkness up to God."[17]

With the quotation above it seems to me that SPR was not founded on a mistake. In the Bible as stated in Acts 5 v. 17ff., the High Priests wanted to kill the disciples, but a Pharisee in the Council named Gamaliel, who was a teacher of the law, said to them "Men of Israel, take care what you do with these men." He related this to Judas the Galilean, who rose to power in the days of census and who was joined by many people. In the end he perished and all his followers were scattered. "So in this present case, I tell you, keep away from these men and let them alone; for if this plan or this undertaking is of men, it will fail; but if it is from God, you will not be able to overthrow them." Based on this argument, the SPR will undoubtedly continue to exist for ever, because God will continue revealing himself to man for his glory. Douglas, A., however, comments in his book, *Extra-Sensory Powers*, that "when the SPR was founded, its purpose was to examine without prejudice in a scientific spirit those faculties of man, real or supposed, which appear to be inexplicable on any generally recognised hypothesis."[18] He adds that "such pre-occupations and interests shaped the form which Psychical Research was to take for decades to come."[19]

An End of My Life

On 13th January, 1993, I visited Malawi to see my mother, who was ill, and returned to England on 8th February. Before I left for England, my mother said to me: "My life is coming to an end, I am glad you came to see me because you will not see my face again." I believed her, because I had been home to see her before on account of her illness, and she had not said anything of the kind. I felt that something must have prompted her to say this to me. I was puzzled and lost for words and became apprehensive. When I returned to England, I narrated the event to my friend Grace Jal-wang, who suggested I should arrange to give my mother a surprise visit to prove her wrong. My friend suggested I should say to my mother, "You said to me on my last visit that you would not see me again; now here I am, and I can see you again."

I also told my other colleagues at work of my plan to visit home before my mother died. One of them had some doubts about the journey, and said: "You have to think about money, Mary." I kept quiet and did not say anything. I felt that my mother was more important to me than money. I could not go home that month in April 1993, because nothing seemed to go according to plan. Although I said openly to my colleagues that I wanted a holiday, I found myself helpless each time I wanted to implement the decision to go home.

Dream 1: My Mother and I Sleeping in My Father's Graveyard

It followed then that on 8th April 1993, between 4.30 and 4.45 a.m., I had a lucid dream which was very vivid. I dreamed that my mother and I were sleeping in a small house. The small house was erected at the precise spot where my father had been buried at our family cemetery. This was a small brick house in the form of a square. The little house appeared to have no doors but I saw my mother come out of it suddenly. When she got up to go out, a door seemed to appear. It was then that I saw brightness outside. The time seemed to be between 2.00 and 3.00 a.m. The moon was shining and the stars seemed brighter than ever, when suddenly my mother got up from where both of us were sleeping, got dressed in her normal clothes, which I had seen her wear when I went home previously, and left me alone in the house.

She told me to stay where we were sleeping while she went to our old kitchen to light the fire. We had stopped using this old kitchen. It had been abandoned even though it was in good condition. This kitchen had been abandoned when our old big house had fallen down and we had to build another house at a different location and another kitchen was built near this new house. We don't use the old kitchen because it is far from the new house.

As she went to light the fire, I saw her carry four maize stalks on her shoulder in a similar manner to the way men would carry firewood at home. Women carry firewood on their heads while the men place it on their shoulders. The maize stalks were dry and she was probably going to use them for the fire. However, as she walked towards the kitchen door, she turned away from the setting sun.

I stood by the door as she walked towards the kitchen and asked whether she was coming back. She kept on saying she was going to the kitchen. She was talking to herself while she was going to the kitchen and did not look back until she reached it. I continued watching her and she disappeared and never came back; I could see her still carrying those four maize stalks until she disappeared. She picked those four maize stalks from our garden. It was in this garden that my father was buried and we were sleeping underneath his grave. This small house was built there. My father's body lay in state in this kitchen when he died. So it seems everything that happened in the dream was following my father's footsteps. I understand that my mother had requested that her body should lie in state in the kitchen where my father's body had lain in state.

After my mother had disappeared, the door closed on its own, but before I started panicking that I was in that small house all by myself, another door on the other side opened. I stood by the door again, still looking in the direction where my mother had gone. Two men were sitting by the door on my left. When this second door opened, it faced in the direction of the house of the chief, Inkos Goman. It was still so bright that one could not help being frightened by it. The brightness was brighter than normal. It was very quiet but I could not even hear the birds singing. The two men sitting by the door were dressed like Christ's disciples and were not sitting the way we would sit, but they were kneeling down. They asked me whom I was looking for and I told them I was looking for my mother. "She has left me on my own, she just said 'bye-bye' as she went to the kitchen. She never came back." The two men who resembled Jesus' disciples said to me: "That's it, she has gone, you will not see her again." They continued saying, "Don't worry, there is nothing to worry about." That was the end of the dream.

After finishing work, I went straight to Grace Jal-wang to tell her of the dream. She kept quiet and refrained from making any comment. Perhaps she did not want to tell me that my mother was definitely going to die. However, she looked sad. The Sunday of the same week, I narrated the dream to another colleague from Uganda. She said: "it seems as if your mother is righteous, she will go to heaven." Perhaps that was another way of telling me my mother was about to die. She was telling me indirectly, I suppose. I also told another colleague at work during lunch hour in the canteen. She gave me a similar reply. I should think these two colleagues were equating the disciples with righteousness. Equally I myself interpreted it to mean the disciples came to protect my mother at her death, especially since both the disciples and myself were where my mother was buried.

However, the dreamer is the best interpreter of the dream. I knew my mother was definitely going to die. She was saying bye-bye to me in this dream. What else could one want to know? I told my friends that the dream prompted me to buy a suitcase ready to travel home. They asked me whether I didn't already

13

have one. When I went home in January, I said that I normally leave my suitcase at home each time I travel there. When I went home in January, I bought two white bed sheets and a pillow case from George Henry Lee's for my mother. This was in preparation for her funeral. I intended to buy perfume as well but forgot. I regretted this when my sister told me they did not have perfume to use when my mother died. They tried some shops but they could not get any. During the same trip, my sister, Sister Victoria, and my brother, Oliver Chinkwita, told me they would need a cow for the funeral. So when I came over, I sent the money to buy the cow and I was informed in a letter that the cow had been bought.

The Journey which did not Materialise

After having the dream on 8th April 1993, I decided to take a holiday. But I did not book in advance, which made it difficult for me. However, one of the colleagues at work said something could be sorted out, even though I had not booked a holiday. My line manager suggested I could have the holiday in June, but I wanted it either in April or in early May, failing which there would be no need for a holiday. He asked me whether I wanted to go home and I said I just wanted a holiday, I just wanted to go to London. I did not know what people's reaction would be if I told them I wanted to go home because of the dream I had had. But I was more open with my friends outside work. Dreams became a subject of discussion for the whole of April and early May 1993. We could share our dreams and make comparisons.

I bought my suitcase, packed everything and went to book my flight. I wanted to travel on 26th April by French Airline UTA but did not have enough money for the journey; it was before we got paid. Although I went to enquire about the travel, I realised I was going to have a problem with the money, since it was before the end of the month. For this reason I told them if they did not see me by Friday, 24th April, it meant we had not been paid. As it was, I failed to travel.

I went to book again to travel on 3rd May. Whilst I was at the travel agent, I realised that Monday the 3rd was a Bank Holiday. I feared I might have some difficulty in travelling to Manchester Airport. For this reason, I gave up and did not go back to the travel agent to confirm the booking. If I had told some colleagues, they would have taken me to the airport, but I am generally shy. On the other hand, I prefer doing things by myself. However, I gave up. I learned in the end that it was possible to leave your car at the airport. But on the other hand, this would have meant paying the airport fee, a thing I could not afford.

Interestingly, I could not stop talking of the dream. I could talk about it but could not go home. However, I wrote a letter to my sister in Zimbabwe. I told her to go home as soon as possible to see my mother. I just said she was very sick. There was no need to talk about the dream in the letter lest she did not believe me. I also wrote to my other sister in Blantyre. She replied that we were all going to meet at home on 26th April. In her own words, "We will all meet there". Unfortunately I did not travel, as has already been stated above. She too did not go on 26th April; instead she sent her daughter.

Dream 2: Burying my own Mother

It was the second time that I booked to travel but could not, because 3rd May was a Bank Holiday. Why I gave up no one knows, only God the Almighty. The girls at the travel agent seemed fed up with me because I continually changed my bookings. Probably they even thought there was something wrong with me. On 3rd May, 1993, at 6.30 a.m., the day I intended to travel, I had another dream. My mother was incontinent, and my sister, Sister Victoria, cleaned her. She put the waste in a big parcel and gave it to me to throw in the toilet. I complained, saying the toilet hole was too small, that the pack could not fit in. I then asked for a hoe. They gave it to me, and I dug a big square hole and put the parcel in the hole. That was the end of the dream.

I felt I should discuss this dream with one of my friends because she had told me of a similar dream. She dreamt of two young children who were incontinent and later two of her relatives died in London. I did not know the exact meaning of this second dream, but the dream left me helpless. Although I did not interpret the dream fully, it was like the final dream about my mother's death. On Tuesday, I went to book a flight on 10th May, reaching Malawi on 11th May, by the French Airline UTA. I actually withdrew the money and gave it to the girl at the travel agents. She counted the money and it was the right amount. The ticket was £545 cheap season, and it was increased to £550 with tax. Sadly, I gave up again for no apparent reason. The girl gave me back the money to keep it in an envelope until she had finished making all the necessary enquiries. After making a long distance phone call, the girl told me to add an extra £10, since it was too late for the ticket to come over by post. The £10 was for sending it by courier. With this I told her point blank that I was not travelling on 10th May because of that extra £10. I told her I did not have the extra £10, and asked her why she had not told me of the extra charge when I was making my enquiries. I had been to the travel agent, A.T. Mays, two or three times prior to this encounter, and they had never mentioned about the extra £10. The girl was very helpful. She asked me to make up the difference by cheque, but I still refused and demanded my money back. Everyone present was surprised. This was inevitably to fulfil my mother's words that I was not going to see her face again. I wonder how on earth anyone could afford to buy the air ticket and yet fail to pay an extra £10.

Back home, however, my sister kept on informing my mother each time I said I was going. But my mother questioned that. She told my sister I was not going. That I changed my mind and decided not to travel on 26th April made her believe strongly I was not going to go. Presumably, she knew this in her heart, as she had already told me that I was not going to see her again.

Although I kept on changing the dates, I nevertheless knew I was still going to travel. For some reason I knew I was going to travel home, but did not know when. I remember having written to one of the tutors at St. Colm's College, asking him not to send me certain books, since I was going to be away and there would be no one to receive the parcel. I asked him to send the books at the end of May. I told him I was going for a holiday, although I did not know when. Why I said the end of May no one knows, only the Almighty. It was as if the future was known to me.

So psychic experience is significant in my life. How I could tell my line manager that I could only have my holiday if it was April or early May, not June, still puzzles me. Equally, how I could tell the tutor that I was going away without actually booking the holiday or the flight still remains a mystery to me. These are not coincidences or chances, but some sort of hidden knowledge in us. Hence "The Angelic Guidance", as I have always maintained.

Another reason why I abandoned booking the plane was that I had not consulted my line manager; I did not feel good about not checking with him first. Equally, I was sure if I had told him that my mother was very sick, and that I had booked the plane, he would have let me go. At the same time, to say she was very sick would also have meant telling a lie. It was my dreams that were telling me she was very sick. At other times she had been sick and sometimes alright. However, I gave up the idea of booking for unknown reasons. Perhaps the idea of me sleeping in the graveyard together with my mother added to my fear of not going home. Although I did not tell anyone, it was still in me that I might be buried together with my mother if I happened to go. The dream contributed considerably to my apathy in not wanting to go home. When I requested my money back, the other girls at the travel agent asked the girl who was dealing with my ticket why I could not travel. I could hear her say that it was because I could not add a further £10. They were all amazed as to how one could afford to pay £550 and fail to pay an extra £10.

However, everything has a motive behind it. In this case the motive was my mother's words, "We will not meet again, this is our last time to see each other." So I decided not to travel on Monday, 10th May in order to reach Malawi on Tuesday, 11th

May. Unfortunately, 10th May was the day my mother died. So if I had travelled I would have seen her dead body at least, since I would have arrived on Tuesday morning, the day my mother was buried. But seeing the body also seemed implausible; to see the dead body would have been the reverse of my mother's words. Some people do perceive things and they happen in that exact manner. Psychic experience is very much stronger. I knew what my mother had said was not implausible. She was generally very quiet. For her to talk meant that what she said was definitely going to happen.

I do recognize, though, that in the dream that informed me about my mother's death, my mother's psychokinesis was much stronger than probability. That which has been perceived cannot be refuted or challenged. I tried to challenge my mother's words, but effort was fruitless. All the struggle I had taken to reach home before she died had failed. Frankly there was no element of illusion in my mother's psychic feelings. No one can challenge this because it is just a plain fact. Thus to my mind, I would say such a power definitely exists in all of us. Some people are prone to extra-sensory perceptions. Everyone experiences them, but I am only evaluating them. There are numerous incidents like this in Africa, but no one has recorded them.

Not Coincidences but God's Manifestation

There are also incidents in which, upon a relative's death, a watch would just stop on its own. For example, J.B. Rhine, as quoted by John Randall, reported just such a case. "During the 1930s one of his girl students told him that her father's clock had stopped at the exact moment of his death, although it was not run down or out of order." A very close friend of mine, Pat Jenkins, shared with me the information that her grandfather's clock had stopped at the moment when he died. She writes in her own words: "My grandfather's clock was too large for the shelf, so it stood ninety years on the floor. It was taller by half than the old man himself, though it weighed not a pennyweight more. It was bought on the morn of the day that he was born, and was always his treasure and pride, but it stopped, never to go again, when the old man died." This coincides with a well known song which goes, "Ninety years without slumbering, tick tock, tick tock." Examples of this sort do happen to us almost daily, only it is hard for some to incorporate paranormal happenings in their lives. These are also meaningful coincidences in themselves; meaningful coincidences because they tell us something.

However, since my plan to go home failed to materialise in time, I kept myself busy writing letters to relatives instead. I wrote to my cousin, and told her my mother was sick and that I was definitely going home. She told her sister, Mrs. Elemin Kamunga. Her sister, upon hearing this, decided to go to see my mother before she died, presumably to see her for the last time. She went and the following week my mother died. She was happy to have found her alive at least for one more week.

Mary's Brain Does not Work

My sister in Zimbabwe was puzzled to receive a letter from me to the effect that our mother was very ill. It would have surprised her less had it originated from relatives in Malawi. She thought it was sheer madness on my part and therefore decided not to act. Even though she disregarded some of the contents of my letter, she decided to make arrangements to go home to meet me, as I had mentioned in my letter that I would be home either at the end of April or in early May. Her efforts to book a seat on the Zimbabwe-Malawi express bus for the 3rd May and 6th May were all in vain, as it was fully booked. My sister afterwards said to her family: "Mary just wants to bother me. She wants me to travel home for no good reason. Who told her mother is dying?" She therefore gave up the idea of going home. On Monday, 10th May, my mother's heart ground to a halt – she passed away. "It is a promising bright Monday morning," or so my sister thought, when she woke up and went about her household chores, until she received a telephone call from Malawi informing her of the untimely death of our dear mother. It suddenly turned into a blue Monday for the entire family. She said to her children: "Look now what has happened, Mary's brain is dangerous." The brain which does not work has become useful. However, she quickly arranged to travel by air the following day. It is a 50-minute flight from Harare and Lilongwe, from where she travelled by car for about an hour to our place, Lizulu. Her daughter in Zimbabwe arranged with someone in Lilongwe to pick her up from Kamazu International Airport to take her to Lizulu. As it was, she managed to attend the funeral ceremony. At least she had a glimpse of my mother's face before she was buried.

Given up the Idea of Travelling

I myself had given up the idea of travelling. I left everything in the hands of God. But then a number of people kept asking me whether I had had my holiday. Had it been August or September, I would have understood, because that's when a lot of people do go on holiday. At a seminar on Friday, 7th May, on 'Equal Opportunities', Mr. V.T. Citarella (Director of Social Services) asked me whether I had had my holiday yet. I told him I had not booked in advance, but I wanted it during the month of May. With him asking me, I felt there must be a reason; he has never asked me about my holidays. Certainly I felt some guardian angels were reminding me to go home.

I concluded my guardian angel was definitely directing me to go for a holiday to see my mother. But why I failed to respond, no one knows. On Saturday, 8th May, in the morning, I went to buy more things to take home, but I hadn't re-booked my flight (which I had cancelled) to travel on 10th May. Nevertheless, I still continued to buy things, of course not knowing when I would travel. The same Saturday, 8th May, in the afternoon, a Canadian writer was coming to give a talk at Toxteth Library, Liverpool 8. His name was Iqbal Ahmad and he came to speak about his latest collection of works, *The Opium Eaters, and Other Stories*. He was supposed to come at 2.00 p.m. but was delayed from starting out by an hour. This gave us the chance to talk to each other. I carried two copies of my book, *The Usefulness of Dreams*. Dreaming, therefore, became a subject of discussion. We found ourselves talking about dreams. I was talking with a girl from Kashmir, a student lawyer. She was sharing her dreams with me. The fascinating one to me was about her immediate uncle; she saw her uncle in a dream saying 'bye-bye' to her, and she wondered where her uncle was going. The following week after the dream her uncle died.

I listened intently. Her dream reminded me of the one I had had in which my mother said goodbye to me. I told her I was supposed to travel on Monday the 10th May, the day after next, but I cancelled the journey for no apparent reason. I told her I had known my mother was going to die, but each time I wanted to go I had found myself powerless and had given up the idea of going. From there I went to Grace Jal-wang's house as usual, and told her about my conversation with this girl, particularly the dream about her uncle.

From Grace's house I went to see a former colleague, Gladys Marriot, whom I worked with at Parkside Hostel, a hostel for people with physical disabilities. She wanted a copy of my previous book. I had brought a copy to give to her. Once again I told her about the two dreams I had had about my mother. She said, "It seems as if God is preparing you for your mother's death." I said 'yes' without any hesitation. She too shared her psychic experience with me. She does not dream, but told me about what she had said to her husband. Her husband had been sick on several occasions and all that time she had never said anything.

"I was just as bad"

It was in 1989 when her husband was taken ill. Before he became ill, she had said to her husband "Will you forgive me for what I have said in the past?" The husband said: "I love you as much as you love me, and I was just as bad." He was taken into the hospital the same week. The following day was 12th August and they were supposed to celebrate their 39th wedding anniversary. She sent him a card and a bottle of wine, with her son. When he reached the hospital the doctor sent him back with a request to bring his mother. The son came to tell his mother that the doctor had sent for her. At this time, the husband was unconscious. When the wife reached the hospital, the doctor told her to talk to her husband. He said that her husband could still hear even though he was unconscious. The wife talked to her husband, and he tapped her three times on the palm and died. The wife interpreted these three taps as "I love you". So the husband died. The wife was amazed and wondered why she asked her husband to forgive her on this occasion, even though he had been ill several times before. It was as if she knew he was going to die.

Still No Sense of Direction

I left Gladys Marriot and went to my house. On Monday, I went to work. In the afternoon I went to Fazakerley for a meeting. The meeting finished at 4.30 p.m. I normally go back to the office, but on this day I decided to go straight home. I went via my friend's house to get some potatoes and carrots for my evening meal. I had only meat in my fridge, so I wanted some potatoes to go with it. My friend asked me to wait for a cup of tea and I said 'no' for the first time. It is our African tradition to have at least something once you enter your friend's house. But on this occasion, Monday, 10th May, my mind was set to go to my house and rest. I came home and began to cook the potatoes, carrots and meat. While these were cooking, the telephone rang and it was my niece telling me my mother had died. The news did not come as a shock, since my mother had already told me and the dreams had also told me. I just said 'okay'. After five minutes, Mr. D. Chikhadzula rang telling me the same thing. I told my niece that they should wait for me and not to bury my mother before my arrival. She said my brother had already said they were not going to wait for anyone. I told Mr. Chikhadzula the same thing and he said "No, we are not going to wait". Apparently my mother's words were to be fulfilled that I was not going to see her face again. May is very cold in Malawi, and no one knows why they were in such a hurry to bury my mother.

However, I immediately stopped cooking my meal. I regretted that I had not gone home. Why had I kept on changing my mind? I felt hopeless and to some extent depressed. Not because she had died, but because now I would not see her before she died. I felt I should give thanks to God, though, that he kept her alive for so long. She died at the age of 93. Also I thanked God that she died a natural death, unlike my father. He was killed thirty years ago. His killing was a great shock to all the family. For this reason I am grateful to the Lord for having looked after my mother for such a long time.

Although I was not myself when my mother died, this was just because we love our dear ones. Even though we are well aware that one has to die when one is old, we don't want to accept it. We just want our parents to live forever with us. Needless to say, on that particular day when my mother died, I wanted to pray to commend her spirit to the Lord, but I could not pray and could not cry. I was indeed not myself. I went to my friend to tell her the bad news, and she said not to worry; even if I had gone on that Monday to arrive home on 11th, I would still have missed the burial as I would have been delayed in town, in Lilongwe, not knowing what had happened. I would not have gone to the village straight away. Something would still have delayed me so as to fulfil my mother's words. If I had travelled on the Monday, I would also have missed the telephone call.

I decided to book my flight to travel on Wednesday, 12th May, by KLM, Dutch Airline. This time I had to pay more than my booking with the French Airline. I paid £575. I had to pay that extra £10 as well. I had no choice this time; I had to go. I left Manchester Airport at 8.00 p.m. on Wednesday, 12th May, and reached home the following day, Thursday, at 11.00 a.m. local time, 9.00 a.m. British time.

Conversation in a Taxi

While going to the Airport, I hired a taxi to take me to the coach station. The taxi driver asked me where I was going and I told him the story of my mother's death. I said I would probably have left a week earlier or on 10th, but kept on changing for no apparent reason. I said perhaps it was still okay since my mother had already said goodbye to me. It was as if she knew the future. The taxi driver commented that his mother too had died. Before she died she told her children that she wanted to go to Australia to see her son's children. The family kept on telling her it was very expensive to go to Australia, but she insisted. The family contributed some money and she was able to travel. She went and came back to Liverpool. She lived only two weeks after she had been to Australia. It shows that people know when they are going to die. This lady anticipated her death subconsciously and so insisted on going to Australia, apparently to see everyone before her death and to say bye- bye. Something was telling her to go and see the children. This too is psychic or perception.

Meeting my Brother and Uncle at the Kamuzu Airport

I arrived in Malawi at 11.00 a.m., as already stated. My brother and my uncle came to meet me at the airport. A colleague gave us a lift and dropped us in town to take a bus to my village, Lizulu. While we were waiting for the bus, my brother went to buy bread and milk. I started relating my dreams to my uncle. He said "All that you have said is there, you will see everything for yourself. We had to cut the maize stalks in order to make a path for people to go to the graveyard." The maize had just dried. He said the maize stalks my mother was carrying in the dream were the maize stalks which they had cut. He also added that they had made a small house where they had buried my mother. And that is the house where my mother and I were apparently sleeping.

My brother had come from buying the milk and bread. We took the bus going home to our village. When we reached home, we

24

found the women still in the house. They were in the kitchen where my mother had said she was going in the dream. As I pointed out earlier, she had requested, before she died, to be kept in that kitchen, because that is the kitchen where my father was kept when he died. That is why my mother wanted her body to be kept in that same kitchen before her burial. All my dreams were becoming a reality.

Uniting with my Family and the Women

I entered the kitchen to join the women. We all started crying. We then stopped crying in order to sing and pray. My mother's favourite song was '378', so it was repeatedly sung. Later on Mai Namoyo prayed and narrated the story of how my mother died. My mother had sent for her. She sent a girl to go and call her before she died. Her village is close to ours. The church minister lives three miles away from us, so it was difficult to get hold of him. Mai Namoyo, however, went quickly to our house upon hearing that my mother wanted her. That was Monday, 10th May, before 1.00 p.m.

When she came, my mother told her she called her to pray for her. Before the prayer, she requested the song, the one which she told them to sing for her when she died. The words are as follows:-

> 1. We live to suffer on earth
>   But God's land is full of blessings.
>   It is where our Lord Jesus went.
>   He went ahead of us.
>   We will all follow him.
>   At the doomsday

> *Chorus*
>   Let us go, let us go
>   To the blessings land.
>   We will definitely reach there
>   On the doomsday

2. We will reach that land
   When our journey will come to an end.
   Our Lord Jesus Christ will make it possible.
   For us to reach there.
   We will not suffer
   In God's land,
   We will be happy forever

After they had finished the song, the lady started to pray. My mother responded to her prayer by saying "mm, mm, mm". Some people say amen, amen, but on this occasion my mother was saying mm, mm, mm. In my language this is just agreeing with what the lady was saying. One normally says this when one is touched with the prayer. Later on my mother stopped responding, and the lady who was praying thought she was listening attentively, not knowing that my mother was already dead. She kept quiet when she realised my mother had died. She said 'amen' quickly. What a wonderful death it was! The lady said we were crying because it is our tradition, otherwise there was no need to cry. She died a peaceful death. She is now at peace with God.

Sharing my two Dreams with the Women

When I arrived home, I found my relatives and other women still in the kitchen where my mother was laid. The lady who said the prayer while my mother was dying related the story again to me. That was after the prayers and all the singing. I told them all my experiences during this period when my mother was struggling with death. I told them too of my dreams; The first one of my mother carrying the maize stalks. They told me I was going to see all the maize stalks there in the garden. I related the second one of my mother being incontinent and myself digging a hole to bury the excrement and covering it with sand. They all exclaimed and said with one voice that I was actually burying my own mother in the dream. I could not interpret it in a similar manner

26

as the women interpreted it before, because I had never associated my digging a hole with digging the grave. I was just too feeble to interpret it. The dream seemed much easier to interpret after the women had said their part. Sometimes one does not reason properly if one is depressed. I cannot deny the element of depression during this period of my mother's suffering. It seemed to me as if the spirits were sending the messages to me. However, after seeing the graveyard, I was more able to understand its interpretation. I had this second dream on the 3rd May, which was the Monday of the week before my mother died. The following week after the dream was the 10th, and the 10th was a Monday – the day my mother died.

I told them also of all my efforts to get home before my mother died. They all said with one voice again that it was not possible because of what my mother had said. They said that when an elderly person says something, she means just that, not anything else. The first dream was very easy for me to interpret because if someone turns his/her back to you that means she is definitely going to die. Her time of living had come to an end.

Visiting my Mother's Graveyard

I told them in the end I was going to the graveyard, but they told me not to, saying I was to go the following day, according to tradition. I refused and insisted on going to the grave that very day. So they sent word to some elders in the village and they all came. We then started for the graveyard. We took a white cloth to put on the graveyard. Upon reaching the grave, I saw the path they had made by cutting maize stalks. And I saw the small house they had constructed, where my mother was buried. The small house had no door, exactly as I had seen it in the dream. When the door had opened after my mother got up, it just meant a door for her to pass through or to enter the graveyard. The door closed after my mother had come out and another one opened; which enabled me to come out too from that small house. When I came out myself, I realised the dream was just separating me from my mother. The door then closed again. Although my mother went out first, saying she was going to make a fire in our kitchen, in real life it was herself who was left in the graveyard. She went along that path walking to the kitchen just to show that people were going to carry her from our kitchen, walking exactly along the path she had walked. After they buried her, however, they erected this house without a door just as I saw it in the dream. However, she was sleeping peacefully there. I was puzzled, realizing that the small road they had made was the exact path my mother was walking when she said she was going to the kitchen. It connected with the other path, the old existing path where people normally pass, and this old path reaches our kitchen where my mother was going.

Not Four but Five

When the new path they had made reached the old one, they took five maize stalks and closed the path so that people should not think that it was the ordinary path. So they had to close it with five maize stalks. And those were the four maize stalks my mother was carrying in the dream. Normally, they would have closed it with tree branches, but on this occasion they used the five maize stalks. I was amazed. The slight difference though was that my mother was carrying four, whereas in the real life situation they had used five. I think sometimes in a dream you miss the exact number. It might well be that my mother was carrying five and I counted four. Presumably I might have unconsciously interpreted the dream but tried to alter it, or the number of stalks.

I had the same feeling as J.W. Dunne, in his book, *An Experiment with Time*. He saw in a dream a mountain explosion killing 4,000 people. When the dream came to reality, the number of people who were actually killed was 40,000 not 4,000. Thus, Dunne stated, "the number of people declared to be killed was not, as I had maintained throughout the dream, 4,000 but 40,000. I was out by nought. But when I read the paper, in my haste, I read that number as 4,000; and, in telling the story subsequently,

I always spoke of that printed figure as having been 4,000; and I did not know it was really 40,000 until I copied out the paragraph fifteen years later."[20] This can be a psychological refusal to accept such a large number of deaths. On the other hand, the exact number does not really matter; what matters most is the content of the dream. I think with Dunne that he missed just one nought. But the whole dream was about the explosion and that it was going to kill many people, which happened. It was the same thing in my dream about my mother carrying four maize stalks, whereas in real life they had to be five. I miscounted, or tried to reject the prophesy.

The issue at stake is the maize stalks. Normally, they put lots and lots of trees to make it difficult for the children to enter the graveyard. It would have been the same with the maize stalks, but they chose to put five only. Bearing this in mind, I tend to think I missed one maize stalk. At home the elderly say: "No matter how bright the moon's light might be, you cannot use it to put a thread in the needle's eye." By the same token, the dream happened during the night although I myself normally dream in the morning, but the fact is my eyes were still tired and closed. Anyway, it was around 3.00 or 4.00 a.m. and the scene was in Malawi, when it was still during the night. The dream was just telling me what was going to happen at her death. People were going to use the maize stalks she was carrying for fire and the maize stalks were going to be used for closing the path. In this respect the dream was very accurate.

It also follows that the fire she mentioned in the dream was actually made by men who were sleeping outside. It was in May, and it was winter time, therefore very cold. It was truly a psychic dream. Every little bit she mentioned just happened as she stated it, without missing the smallest detail. Perhaps those who take things as a coincidence would say it was only a coincidence; to me my mother definitely demonstrated everything which was going to happen to her in a dream. So there is a meaning behind this, not just a coincidence.

Real Red Flowers

They showed me inside the graveyard where they had put a few red flowers, thereby reflecting one of the dreams I have had before, and which I have described in *The Usefulness of Dreams: An African Perspective*. I dreamed my mother died and there were so many people that I said to myself in the dream: "What is this? Is this the death of the Queen?" The coffin was covered with red flowers, and immediately my memory flashed back to that dream. I was told there were many people, What I said in the dream was actually said by my uncle, Mr. T. Chipezaani. He told me there were many people, and everyone wondered as to why that was. "One would think it was the death of a queen. People came from all over the country," he said. The women I found at the house upon my arrival also commented on the very same point. They told me many people came to the funeral.

While we were at the graveyard, the village headman preached. In short, he said this was a good death, my mother had lived well with people. Her death was an example to us who were left behind to live a good life. If we don't repent in order to die like her, it's up to us.

He said he had never seen a death where someone actually knows she is dying and says 'bye-bye' to people. He said we were crying because we loved her, otherwise there was no need to cry. She was in heaven with the Lord. He said we knew where she had gone. He pleaded that we live a good life in order to die in the same manner.

Walking in the Valleys and Mountains

Mrs. Margaret Chikhadzula came to see me the very same week I arrived. I related the first dream, in which my mother said good-bye to me. She commented that "The day before my mother died, I had a similar kind of dream. My mother and I were walking in mountains and valleys. It was all green. We would walk and stop. Eventually, we came to a river and my mother repeatedly told me to stand where I was while she crossed the river, leaving me alone. That was the end of the dream. The day after this dream my mother died." By coincidence, her mother, like my mother, said bye-bye to her in a dream and in real life. All the things her mother was telling her made her believe her time had finished.

Incidentally, I was very close to Mrs. Chikhadzula's mother. I went to visit Malawi one year before she died, and decided to call on her. Her mother and I had beds in one room, and we did not sleep that night. She was telling me her time had ended. She wanted to give me a land where my family could grow maize, beans, ground-nuts and other vegetables. She said that the best time for me to get a place was while she was still alive. She insisted I would not get a place if I did not act during that holiday. I was not ready for the offer on that holiday; I thought I was going to go again for another holiday. On the other hand, I was questioning in my heart how she knew she was going to die. I thought she just wanted me to get land at that time. Not long afterwards, when I returned to Britain, I heard she died. I was full of regrets.

It seems to me that those who die in Christ do know the time of their death. We went to Sybil Holmer's funeral on 10th August 1994. Sybil was a Presbyterian and worked in Taiwan as a nurse for 25 years. She was very active there in Taiwan. She also helped with the teaching of English. She was very active in Liverpool at the church, and she helped many foreigners, of which I was one. At the church during her funeral, the minister said Sybil knew she was dying. She thanked her sister with whom she was staying before she went to bed the night she died. She said to her sister "Thank you for being good to me and for your great help." She said this before going to bed. Sybil died in her sleep. I was with a family from Ghana at the funeral, and when we were going to the cremation, the wife asked whether Sybil was sick. I said 'no' she wasn't; she died in her sleep. She asked how, in that case, she had known she was dying, to cause her to say bye-bye to her sister. The husband replied saying, "Those who live with God, the same God makes them know when they are dying." In other words the Lord reveals the day of their death.

However, both Mrs. Chikhadzula and myself found it very fascinating that our mother actually said bye-bye to us both through dreams and in a real-life situation. We also talked of how righteous our parents were, and that they looked forward to their deaths, presumably to follow their husbands or to be with our dear Lord. That they looked forward to their deaths is an encouragement to us.

Spending Time in Prayers

The whole of my stay at home was spent in prayers in which we encouraged each other. We alternated in our prayers. My brother, Stensfield, one day reminded us of the words of Paul in I. Thessalonians 4 vs 14-17 RSV. "For since we believe that Jesus died and rose again, even so, through Jesus, God will bring with him those who have fallen asleep. For this we declare to you by the word of the Lord that we who are alive, who are left until the coming of the Lord, shall not precede those who have fallen asleep. For the Lord himself will descend from heaven with a cry of command, with the sound of the archangel's call, and with the sound of the trumpet of God. And the dead in Christ will rise first; then we who are alive, who are left, shall be caught up together with them in the clouds to meet the Lord in the air; and so we shall always be with the Lord."

The historical fact of the resurrection of Christ is the basis of Christian hope in life beyond death. This translation implies that at the Parousia God will, by the power of Jesus, bring the dead back to life. 1 Cor. 6v. 14: "And God raised the Lord and will also raise us by his power." RSV.

Peake's commentary on the Bible, by Matthew Black et al., states that "...the substance of the tradition, based on the words and works of Jesus, illuminated by the O.T. and handed on by the missionaries in their campaigns, was regarded as having divine authority[21], i.e. the words of the Apostle Paul, "We who are alive".

1 Thessalonians 4 v. 15. At the time Paul thought he was going to live until the Parousia. But with his illness, he changed his belief that he was still going to be alive by the time the Lord comes. 2 Corinthians 1 vs 8-9. And also Philippians 1 v 20 RSV. "As it is my eager expectation and hope that I shall not be at all ashamed, but that with full courage now always Christ will be honoured in my body, whether by life or by death."

Paul's intention, as Peake's commentary states, was to comfort the Thessalonians, not to supply a literal description of the end of the world. The last words of v.16 and 17 in 1 Thessalonians 4 provide the assurance for which the Thessalonians had asked. They also contain what is probably the only original Pauline teaching in this passage, that those who die 'in Christ' before his final Triumph remain 'in Christ' until they are welcomed into his presence to be with him forever.[22] The picture is that of the end of the world. The passage carries the O.T. allusions and images derived from descriptions of the descent to earth of God in judgement as depicted by the prophet. The dead will rise as in Daniel 12: v 2: in Isaiah 27: v 19a, and the living will be gathered up as in Isa 27: 12b, 13a.

By coincidence, the passage above was my mother's favourite. I used to see her reading about what Paul had said about the last day. That those who are still alive will meet with the dead in heaven. We will rise in a minute to meet with the Lord on hearing the trumpet (lipenga). Then she would start preaching to us. My brother did not know this since he did not live with us. My father sent him to a mission boarding school while young, and he used to stay there even during the holidays. So he chose the passage, not on account of the fact that my mother liked it, but because it is his favourite passage too. This was not just a coincidence in itself, but more than a coincidence.

There are presumably many psychic experiences similar to my mother's case, only no one recorded them. My mother's psychic experience, however, was justified. My sister, who died in 1995, and my friend's mother knew subconsciously that they were going to die.

My Sister's Death – February 1995

In addition to my mother, my sister, who had lived in Zimbabwe since 1949, had an experience similar to hers. Unlike my mother, my sister only knew subconsciously. My mother's case was straightforward. To this end she was able to say goodbye to me and to the rest of the family.

My sister did the same. Only in her case, she herself didn't know where she was going. She thought she was going to Johannesberg (South Africa), when in actual fact she was going to join her mother. It was less than two years after my mother had died when my sister died. She herself and her friend regularly visited Johannesberg for selling and buying goods. She never said bye-bye to her neighbours each time she went to South Africa. But on this occasion she went from door to door saying goodbye to all her friends and neighbours. In her own words, "I have already packed; I am going to Joberg tomorrow." Ndakagadzila packed blankets etc. Her friends were surprised and said to themselves "She always goes there and she never came to say bye-bye to us before, why this time?" Some thought she was just happy to say bye-bye on this occasion. She was travelling on a Thursday and it was Wednesday when she said bye-bye to all those who were close to her.

The goodbye did not end there. After going round, she assembled all her children. She waited for those children who went to work. When everyone had come, she cooked and ate together with them. She told them they had to sing church songs and pray together. In fact they sang until 12.00 midnight. They repeated the same song all through, 347 in our church hymnal. It goes:

> 1. Father, I am your son/daughter
>   Although I sinned,
>   I cry unto thee:
>   Forgive my sins!

Chorus
>My sins are many,
>That they cannot be counted.
>I look to thee Lord,
>Forgive me.

2. I sinned in thought
   And in my speeches
   And in my deeds.
   Forgive me.

3. I disobeyed,
   I despised you,
   I failed in my deeds.
   Forgive me.

4. All that I liked doing
   Were in vain/nonsense.
   I was not satisfied with my deeds.
   Forgive me.

After the above song, she prayed and told the children to disperse. In the morning she got up and began to get ready to go to South Africa. She went to have a bath. After the bath she came back into the room and called to her husband that she was dying, and she died.

Her husband did not understand. He sent the children to call my sister's friend, who was travelling with her to Johannesberg. The lady, upon seeing the children, started telling them she was coming, she was finishing a cup of tea. The children went closer and said "We have come to tell you that she has died." She left the cup of tea and rushed to see my sister. She confirmed she had died. They called the 'ambulance', which took her to the hospital, but did not find any cause of her death.

She did not know directly she was going to die. But the spirits guided her. By implication she thought she was going to South

Africa, when in reality she was going to the other world. This psychic awareness had been in her for long, I suppose. She went to Zimbabwe in 1949, and since then she had never been to Malawi to stay more than two months. Strangely, she stayed long this time. She went for a holiday in October 1994, and stayed for three months. She returned to Zimbabwe in December, and died in February the following year. It was as if she went to say bye-bye to everyone even though she did not know that she had only two months left to live.

Like my mother, who died in 1993, thousands and thousands of people came to my sister's funeral. As in my mother's case, I missed the funeral. However, I managed to see the video. At the funeral, the church minister continued singing my sister's song which she sang almost the whole night before she died. It was indeed a peaceful death, like my mother's. She asked for forgiveness and I believe the Lord did forgive her. The Psalmist cried to the Lord, "Purge me with hyssop, and I shall be clean; wash me, and I shall be whiter than snow. Fill me with joy and gladness; let the bones which thou hast broken rejoice. Hide my face from my sins, and blot out all my iniquities." Psalm 51: vs 7-9. RSV.

Regret for Failing to Heed Mother's words

A colleague at work, Mrs. Nargis Anwar, told me of how her mother wanted her to come to see her, but Nargis did not go. She writes in her own words: "My brother was getting married on 27th May 1982 in Pakistan. My mother phoned me from Pakistan a week before the wedding, insisting that I should attend the wedding. I said to her that I could not go because of my new job and for financial reasons as well. She asked me to come for just one week. I told her I did not want to go all that way for just one week, and I promised her that I would visit her in December (1982) and stay with her for at least a month, and that I would also take my two children with me to see her. She got really annoyed and insisted that if I could not make it, I should send my daughter, who was 13 at the time, to attend the wedding. She also said that she would be pleased to see her and then she would not miss me at the wedding. I told her that I could not do that as it was in the middle of a school term. I would not allow her to miss school. She got really angry. I tried my best to calm her down and make her understand, but she slammed the phone down on me. Before she did that she said to me: 'You will regret this as you will never be able to see my face again'. I did not think much of that at the time. I knew she was very temperamental and emotional, but she would come round and would ring me back after the wedding.

"A week later, the day after the wedding, I tried to phone her but could not get through. The wedding was taking place nearly 600 miles away from my home city. I thought that probably they had not returned home from it. But what had actually happened was that she had died on the day of the wedding, soon after the ceremony. My brothers had to bring her body back to Karachi to bury her by my father's side (he was buried in Karachi, my home city). My brother phoned me to give me the bad news. Then I remembered my mother's last words on the phone and I rushed off to Pakistan on the first available flight, but it was too late. She was already buried and I did not see her face again. Her last words had come true. It's nearly 11 years ago and I regret to this day that I did not go to see her."

Contact with the Spirit World

Writing about psychic experience, Ursula Roberts says: "I have lived with such frequent contacts with what is called the 'Spirit World' (or realm of Spirits) that I regard such contacts as part of God's wise provision for guidance in my life."[23] This is in agreement with what I have always maintained. These psychic experiences come to us to strengthen us and to show us our destiny.

Ursula Roberts also related her experiences concerning the spirit of her mother, who died a while ago. She was awakened for ten consecutive nights by a strong scent of sweet peas. She would get up and search the room in order to discover the source of the scent, but all in vain. "On the tenth night the spirit of my mother appeared, looking younger and radiantly happy, and gently kissed me, as if to say goodbye. Since that time the beautiful perfume has never invaded my consciousness."[24] This encouraged Ursula Roberts to know her mother's destiny, and the beautiful flowers and pleasant scent symbolized the heavenly world.

I had a similar dream about my mother, who died as already indicated. I came to England at the end of May, after my mother had been buried, and in August I had this dream. There was a big house built with bricks. The house was not painted so it was easy for me to see the bricks. The house was surrounded by beautiful flowers, which were in the form of trees. The flowers were beautiful; I have never seen such a beautiful combination of flowers before. The house had a fence, but even so I could see everything inside the fence. It was beautiful. The flowers covered the gate. My mother was sitting by the gate. Yet again the fact that she was outside the gate frightened me. Why was my mother not inside the building or inside the gate? As usual I related the dream to a friend, but before I had finished, upon hearing of flowers, my friend exclaimed: "Oh, that means your mother is in heaven." At that time she had just lost her sister and she wished she could have a dream to give her an insight as to where her sister was. I comforted her by saying that not all of us dream, but even if we do dream, it does not mean that the person who died was in hell or in heaven.

However, flowers seem to be an explanation of what heaven is like. I had a dream about my sister who died in 1973. She was very religious, a very devoted Christian. In the dream she too was surrounded by flowers, really beautiful flowers. I pointed this out in *The Usefulness of Dreams*. The yard of the house, the way flowers were arranged, looked also like one of the houses I had seen in Blantyre (Malawi). What struck me most in this dream about my sister was, again, the beauty of the flowers. I could tell my sister was somewhere nice.

38

God has his own ways of showing us the future. As I was told of my mother's death through dreams, Ursula Roberts was told of her husband's death through dreams. She writes, "Firstly, I saw the spirit of his dead brother behind his shoulder and received the thought: 'I am waiting for him'."[25] She appreciated knowing that her husband's brother was going to welcome her husband. She thought perhaps the death was going to happen in the future, but in a few weeks the same spirit appeared to her again and "dropped over my head the semblance of a black veil." She interpreted this to mean she was going to become a widow. This experience helped her to pray for the strength to cope with future difficulties. Thus she states, "Many psychic happenings are of a mundane nature, but they remind me that, in the smallest manifestation of events, spirit is actively concerned, especially when one's welfare and safety are concerned."[26]

Brian Inglis in *The Unknown Guest* 1987, relates Samuel Wilberforce's experience, which happened in 1847. Thus he states: "On 10th February, 1847, Samuel Wilberforce, newly appointed bishop of Oxford, was conferring with some of his clergy when he suddenly exclaimed, 'I am certain that something has happened to one of my sons'.[27] His son Herbert, it later transpired, had been injured in an accident on board a ship at the time. 'I was so possessed with the depressing consequence of some evil befalling him,' Wilberforce wrote to tell his sister, 'that I was unable to shake off the impression.'"

Brian Inglis then states: "In this case there was nothing that the bishop could have done; but it is one of many cases in which the recipient of a distress signal of this kind would have reacted promptly, had it been possible to help. Sometimes a recipient has reacted promptly and, as it turns out, unnecessarily."[28]

Probably the time Wilberforce made this statement was the exact time his son was injured. In this case it was Wilberforce's guiding angel telling him his son had been injured. Hitherto, like dreams, psychic phenomena have been the most important and impressive way in which the superconscious mind possesses its information. Psychic phenomena have helped most people to know their destiny, as in the case of my mother. She definitely knew of it. The song she requested before she died referred to her destiny as revealed in the experiences I have shown in this chapter. It cannot be refuted that it was the power of God revealing himself in his people. God manifests himself in different ways, be it dreams, psychic messages or telepathy. Actually psychic power and telepathy do definitely overlap. I would regard Wilberforce's experience as telepathy.

True Self

I found, however, my mother's psychic very exciting and very unusual. They came purely from within her heart. Although the behaviourists would ascribe any original idea to pure chance, it was a true self, not a chance. Single cases are not usually taken seriously. To this end Koestler argued that "The history of science teaches that most discoveries were made by several people independently from each other, at more or less the same time, and this fact alone (apart from all other considerations) is sufficient to show that when the conditions for an invention or discovery have arrived, the favourable chance event which sparks it off is bound to occur sooner or later."[29] Koestler added that "fortune favours the prepared mind".[30] This phrase was written by Pasteur.

My mother's emotions compelled her to reveal her feelings. As Arthur Koestler has also stated, "A conspicuous feature of all emotions is the feeling of pleasantness or unpleasantness attached to them, usually called their 'hedonic tone'. Freud thought that pleasure is derived from 'the diminution, lowering, or extinction, of psychic excitation and 'un-pleasure (unlust, discomfort, as distinct from physical pain) from an increase of it."[31] From my mother's song, as I have shown earlier, I can see that my mother was in agony. Koestler also stated that "emotion and thought remain united".[32] The various causes which may lead to an overflow of tears – aesthetic or religious rapture, bereavement, joy, sympathy, self pity – all have this basic element in common: a craving to transcend the island boundaries of the individual, to enter into a symbiotic communion with a human being, living or dead, or some higher entity, real or imaginary, of which the self is felt to be part."[33]

Koestler calls the self-transcending emotions the stepchildren of psychology, but they are as rooted in biology as their opposites. Freud and Piaget emphasised the point that a young child does not differentiate between ego and environment. The child is aware of events but does not see itself as a separate entity. "It lives in a state of mental symbiosis with the outer world, a continuation of the biological symbiosis in the womb. The universe is focused on the self and the self is the universe – a condition which Piaget called 'protoplasmic' or 'symbiotic' consciousness."[34] This is likened to a fluid universe, "traversed by the tidal rise and fall of physiological needs, and by minor storms which come and go without leaving solid traces".[35] Then "Gradually the floods recede, and the first islands of objective reality emerge; the contours grow firmer and sharper; the islands grow into continents, the dry territories of reality are mapped out; but side by side with it the liquid world coexists, surrounding it, interpenetrating it by canals and inland lakes, the vestigial relics of the erstwhile symbiotic communion – the origin of that 'oceanic feeling' which the artist and the mystic strive to recapture on a higher level of development, at a higher level of the spiral."[36] Koestler adds that "symbiotic consciousness is never completely defeated".

Conclusion

I have, in this chapter, tried to show the difficulties encountered by people who started psychic research, the debate which went on both for and against. Despite all these disputes, the researchers still continued. The research was done both by individuals and universities. Psychical research is now acceptably known as parapsychology.

I have tried to define the concept of psychic phenomena and

41

through my observation found that psychic phenomena overlap with other claimed phenomena investigated by para-psychologists, such as telepathy, precognition and psychokinesis, as we shall see in the following chapter. Some have regarded it as a natural phenomenon bestowed by God himself and that it should be used to his glory.

I have outlined the two dreams which I had concerning my mother's death. Dream 1: in which my mother and I were sleeping under my father's graveyard, and later in the middle of this dream my mother says bye-bye in the same manner as she did in her real-life situation. She repeated the same words she had spoken to me in February when I went to visit her, before she died in May. It was as though her words were implanted in me and I ended up dreaming of seeing her saying bye-bye, in the very same clothes which she was wearing when she said bye-bye to me. I relate this to what Adler, an American psychologist, pointed out. He was under the impression that waking thoughts are similar to sleeping ones, and in that case dreams are a continuation of our waking life. He believed dreams emanate from within. What you see on the T.V. is the thing you will end up dreaming.

Dream 2: This dream was about burying my own mother. I had this dream on Monday, 3rd May, 1993. The following Monday my mother died. All this could be the memory of what we do at home when someone dies. We dig the ground and bury the dead person. This too supports the Adelian school of thought. Most of my dreams go along with the Jungian school of thought, but on this occasion they indeed supported Adler. In this case I could say that all three psychologists, Freud, Jung and Adler, spoke about their experiences. Freud, in his publication with Dr. Joseph Breuer, called *Studies in Hysteria*, sought to show that physical symptoms of hysteria have their root cause in highly emotional experiences of early life which have been 'repressed' into the unconscious mind and are not recoverable to conscious memory.

In his later work Freud taught that the super-ego of man was frequently in conflict with the id, and that this conflict induced the neurotic state. The super-ego might roughly be called conscience, and the id, desire. The 'id' is the primeval self underneath our conventional good manners built up through civilising influences and the standards inculcated at the outset. The id is then a moral instinctive self and its energy is that of instincts constantly demanding crude expression.

The super-ego is in every person in conflict with the id, but if the conflict rages in the unconscious, and if for instance, the super-ego is inflated by the undeserved esteem of the public, the person is like one who inhabits a room, on the ceiling of which the super-ego in the attic knocks, demanding that the person shall come up, and on the floor of which the id in the cellar knocks, demanding that the person shall come down and respond to its needs, so that the person is distracted and torn asunder.

This ego is weak at first, but can become integrated and organised to face life successfully, deriving its energies from the id and the super-ego as it learns to control them. The id remains primitive and unorganised and the super-ego impossible of attainment. Its demands produce that sense of exaggerated and pathological guilt which is so marked a feature of so many neuroses.

Freud typically thinks that the high sex desire in the child is the main cause of his developing this super-ego. In both the interpretation of dreams, and in his introductory lectures on psycho-analysis 1922, Freud made much of the love of the male child for his mother. In addition to his work on the id, the ego and the super-ego, and his ideas on repressed libido and wish-fulfilment, Freud, as Soozi Holbeche (1991) puts it, "also introduced the world to the Oedipus Complex and the Freudian slip – the slip of the tongue that reveals a hidden and often unpalatable truth".

I have also shown in this chapter my sister's psychic. Unlike my mother, my sister said bye-bye to everyone, saying she was going to South Africa when she was in actual fact dying. My mother knew her destiny very well, whilst my sister's destiny was to some extent hidden. I wonder why? But her song, as I have shown, indicated that subconsciously she knew she was going to die. Both my sister's and my mother's predictions could be categorised as precognition, if precognition means direct access to information about future happenings.

As I have shown in this chapter, this psychic claim phenomenon is also related to telepathy, as in the case of Samuel Wilberforce's experience. I have also indicated what Freud said on feelings, i.e. pleasant and unpleasant. This leads us to the definition of parapsychology, coincidence etc.

Bibliography

1. Hurkos, P., *Psychic*, p. 9, by Wheaton & Co. Ltd, Great Britain 1961/62.
2. Perry, M., *Psychic Studies (A Christian View)*, p. 7, The Aquarian Press: Great Britain 1984.
3. Ibid p. 7.
4. Inglis, B., *The Paranormal, An Encyclopedia of Psychic Phenomena*, p. 14, Granada, London, N.Y., 1985.
5. Ibid p. 15.
6. Ibid p. 15.
7. Ibid p. 15.
8. Ibid p. 15.
9. Ibid p. 16.
10. Ibid p. 16.
11. Ibid p. 16.
12. Ibid p. 17.
13. Marks, D., et al., *The Psychology of The Psychic*, p. 4, Prometheus Books, Buffalo, New York, 1980.
14. Perry, M., op. cit. p. 9.
15. Ibid. p. 9.
16. Ibid. p. 10.
17. Douglas, A., "Extra Sensory Powers", p. 12, *A Century of Psychical Research*, by Victor Gollancz Ltd, London, 1976.
18. Ibid p. 12.

19. Ibid. p. 12.
20. Dunne, J.W., *An Experiment With Time*, p. 49, Faber & Faber Ltd, London, 1934.
21. Black, M., et al., *Peake's Commentary on the Bible*, p. 999, Hong Kong, 1962.
22. Ibid p. 999.
23. Roberts, U., *Quarterly Review Of The Churches Fellowship For Psychical & Spiritual Studies*, Spring 1993, No. 155, p. 13.
24. Ibid p. 15.
25. Ibid p. 15.
26. Ibid p. 15.
27. Inglis, B., *This Unknown Quest*, p. 106-7, Chatto & Windus, London, 1987.
28. Ibid. p. 107.
29. Koestler, A., *The Ghost in the Machine*, p. 156, Hutchinson of London, 1967.
30. Ibid p. 226.
31. Ibid p. 191.
32. Ibid p. 191.
33. Ibid p. 191.
34. Ibid p. 191.
35. Ibid p. 191/2.
36. Ibid p. 191/2.

CHAPTER 2

Definitions and Basic Problems

R esearchers in the field of parapsychology have been faced
with the problem of verification. Research carried out in
the laboratory seems to be more accepted than the
spontaneous phenomena which happen in our daily lives. Those
events which occur in day-to-day life are usually known as
'anecdotal material' because they are difficult to verify, since they
are subjective. They are not regarded as fully scientific evidence.
But I regard those which are subjective as more convincing than
those carried out in the laboratory. In my opinion, the laboratory
evidence is, in most cases, based on probability. On the other
hand, spontaneous events have a degree of confirmation, in
which case they are empirical and are closely connected with the
statistical concept of probability. They are to some extent
scientific, because they deal with facts in real-life situations.

Parapsychology Defined

A number of parapsychological phenomena involve a person
allegedly coming to know something by means other than
reasoning, memory, sense, perception or some combination of
these. Campbell, in 1972, argued, as Flew puts it, that "Parapsychological phenomena, by definition, demonstrate capacities
of mind which exceed any capacities of the brain. They are

receptive only to information which arrives by neural pathways, and so is confined to perception by way of the senses. If some people can learn more about distant, hidden or future facts than memory and influence from present sense perception can teach them, then their minds are not just brains."[1]

The parapsychological phenomena fall into two classes; those in which the mind comes to be in some state by paranormal means, and those in which the mind causes something else to come to be in some state by paranormal means. Parapsychology is defined as "the study of the psi phenomena". Psi is the name of the initial letter of the Greek word from which 'psychic' is derived. It is also right and proper to mention that psi-phenomena are divided into two categories, namely, psi-gamma and psi-kappa. These two words are also from Greek letters, and are respectively concerned with knowledge and movement. Psi-gamma means seeing something without being told, but just knowing by extra-sensory-perception or by a sixth sense. This covers words like clairvoyance or telepathy. By contrast, the word psi-kappa refers to PK (psychokinesis) meaning "influence of the human mind, by direct action of will, on another person, object, or event, not mediated by any physical force yet known."[2]

Equally, if apprehension of knowledge or information only refers to the future, the psychologists would refer to this as paranormal precognition or precognitive psi-gamma. Psi-gamma sometimes refers to simultaneous happenings, that is if adjectives such as 'paranormal retrocognition' and 'retrocognitive psi-gamma' are not employed. As Flew puts it, "When there is no such qualifying adjective we take it that the psi-gamma is neither precognitive nor retrocognitive but simultaneous."[3] It is also right to mention that these words, psi-gamma and psi-kappa, are used only when it is known that the information was not obtained or transmitted by means of any mechanisms or by any means of reasoning, but rather that the information was in a form of intuition.

It is necessary to examine the assumption that psi-gamma is considered as a kind of perception or that it is to be understood with the help of the perceptual model, as J.B. Rhine maintained and propounded in the thirties. Flew is of the opinion that if the word 'extra' in the expression 'extra-sensory', is interpreted as meaning 'outside of and apart from', then that expression becomes a self-contradiction. 'Extra-sensory-perception' then is 'extra-perceptual perception'. So each phrase is just as much of a nonsense as the other. Flew goes on to say, "But if, on the other hand, 'extra-sensory' is interpreted as referring to a hypothetical additional sense, then that hypothesis is at once falsified by two decisive deficiencies."[4] Flew then finds some loop-holes with the Greek expression psi-gamma. In the first instance the subjects who give such knowledge fail to recognise "the deliverance of this supposed new sense." Secondly, "It is at least not obvious that in psi-gamma cases the availability of the information to be acquired in the supposed source really is a causally necessary condition of its acquisition by the clairvoyant or telepathic subject."[5]

Field Presentation

The most important thing is to establish first what is feasible in a normal real-life perception. For example, if I say, "There is a lion", that in itself should be agreed by the principle of verification. Equally, many philosophers hold that verification should be accompanied by a degree of confirmation. In this case the lion ought to be there. It follows then that to say you have seen a lion, be it in a dream, vision or if it is synchronistic, others must see it at the same time. It would seem to raise the question of doubts if others have not seen it. To this end Flew asserts that "The visual perceiver must be having appropriate visual sense data. We might perhaps admit unconscious perception as a peripheral possibility; but standard, central not marginal, mainstream cases must be, surely, those in which the perceiver is immediately aware of some mind-independent reality."[6]

Flew mentions two important points: "The presence of the thing perceived has to be causally necessary to the perceiving;

while the perceiver must be acquiring experiences of, and information about, the objects perceived through the employment of the appropriate sense-organs."[7] This is in accordance with what Dunne, in his book, *An Experiment with Time* (p. 26-27), calls a 'field of presentation', where all psi phenomena, such as dreams, visions, precognition, psychokinesis and psychronicity, are located within the individual's private 'field of presentation'. This field of presentation contains, at any given instant of time, all the phenomena which happen to be offered for possible observation.

Dunne gives an example of reading a book, when one's field of presentation contains the visual phenomena connected with the printed letters of the word one is regarding, and at the same time, contains the visual phenomenon pertaining to the little numeral at the bottom of the page. One fails to take any note of this, but the numeral was clearly in one's vision. "It was affecting your brain via the eye, its psychical 'correlate' was being offered to your attention."[8]

Perhaps psi-gamma ought to be labelled as belief since its knowledge is not through the normal senses. Because of this, some philosophers regard psi-gamma as either cognitive or perceptive, or both. The information acquired through telepathy or clairvoyance could be attributed to chance, since these do not correspond to dreams, visions and imagination. If it is attributed to chance, then the question of perception or unconsciousness is ruled out as well. There is also the assumption that where there could not be perception, there could not be 'extra-sensory perception' either. Thus, Flew asserts that, "It is assumed too often and too easily that 'psi' not only can be, but has to be, attributed to something immaterial, incorporeal, and non-physical; mainly for no better reason than that it is, or would be, non-physical in the quite different sense of being outside the scope of today's physical theories."[9] Flew adds: "Yet the truth is that the very concepts of psi are just as much involved with the human body as are those of other human capacities and activities."[10] Flew quotes the philosopher Wittgenstein, who declared in 1953 that "The human body is the best picture of the human soul".

This relates also to the theory of 'Animists', which states that in these experiences there is an observer and that observer is nothing but a non-entity, or 'conscious automaton'. As Dunne puts it, "He is a 'soul' with powers of intervention which enable him to alter the course of observed events – a mind which not only reads the brain, but which employs it as a tool. Much as the owner of an automatic piano may either listen to its playing or play on it himself"[11]

The Four Basic Phenomena claimed in Parapsychology

In essence there are four basic claimed concepts which the parapsychologists attempt to evaluate: telepathy, clairvoyance, precognition and psychokinesis (PK). Useful explanations are given by Professor Robert Morris, Koestler Chair, at the University of Edinburgh.

Telepathy

The claim that "one individual can become aware of the thoughts or experience of another, in some direct way not involving deployment of currently understood mechanisms for acquiring and processing information".[12] Telepathy "seems to require direct mental interaction of some sort, with no physical interaction apparently needed, and raises the possibility that such exchanges really do represent instances of some sort of 'mind stuff' transcending physical boundaries to get on with business more directly."[13]

Clairvoyance

The claim that "an individual can acquire information directly about remote physical events, once again without access to currently understood mechanisms."[14] Clairvoyance, on the other hand, seems much more analogous to sensory interaction. A physical source of information is detected by the individual, perhaps physiologically, and has an impact upon experiences and behaviour just like our more familiar sensing devices. Thus, it is harder to construe clairvoyance in support of a mind apart from the physical body.[15]

Precognition

Precognition is the claim that "individuals can occasionally get direct access to information about future events, physical or mental, without recourse to rational inference."[16] Morris adds that "Telepathy, clairvoyance and precognition can all be considered as making claims as examples of extra-sensory perception, or ESP, ability. ESP refers to any circumstances in which the individual appears to acquire information from some aspect of the environment, or be influenced by it, in ways that we do not understand within our present science-based framework of knowledge."[17]

Psychokinesis

The other phenomenon which parapsychologists investigate is psychokinesis (PK) or mind over matter. Morris defines PK as involving "the claim that individuals can, on occasion, exert some sort of direct mental influence on physical events, to affect their behaviour or likelihood of occurrence."[18] He goes on to say "if ESP is extrasensory, PK is extra-motor." He further adds that "PK is intriguing yet problematic because it suggests that certain mental (or psychobiological) activities may involve the deployment of some form of energy other than those with which we are known as Psi: a claimed set of abilities or skills to which we apply the adjective psychic, as in psychic ability, being psychic, psychic event, and so on."[19]

In this book I have attributed all my experiences to something

51

which is non-physical, and this non-physical element I have defined as 'Angelic Guidance', although I am well aware that parapsychology is a field of an inquiry. This angelic guidance could be regarded by some as a 'soul' and the soul, to my mind, is the spirit and that spirit is God himself, manifesting in human beings or revealing his knowledge to us. In some cases psi phenomena can be negative but this does not rule out the fact that they happen. I think it is all to do with the question of accepting them or verifying them. Some hold that, as Flew puts it, "A phenomenon is, by definition, paranormal if it contravenes some fundamental and well founded assumption of science."[20] In this sense one could say psi phenomena, be they dreams, visions, telepathy, clairvoyance, precognitive or psychokinesis (PK), are in the category of science since they are based on observation or experience. Philosophically it is believed that a particular hypothesis is said to be confirmed to some degree by a certain amount of evidence. The concept of degree of confirmation is closely connected with, or perhaps identical to, the statistical concept of probability.

Flew, while accepting that psi-gamma is negatively defined, argues that, once it is clearly defined, it turns out to be essentially a statistical notion. Thus he states, "These two conceptual contentions help to account for the fact that no one seems to have been able to think up any even halfway presentable theory to account for the occurrence of psi-gamma, if indeed it does occur."[21] This deficiency, he perceives, 'bears on the question of the scientific status of parapsychology in two ways. For a theory that related the putative psi-phenomena to something else less contentious would tend both to make probable their actual occurrence and to explain why they do thus indeed occur."[22] For example, in Jung's 'Synchronicity', the appearance of a scarab at the exact time when his patient mentioned it had a meaning. It came at the time when his patient was struggling to explain what sort of insect it was in her dream. It was very helpful because the woman did not have the problem of describing it. Equally a scarab is an insect which can be used for healing. So it was helpful and meaningful.

Synchronicity and Coincidence

Synchronicity means two events happening at the same time, in other words, the occurrence of two events together. Jung wrote a famous and controversial essay on this topic, and gave it a subtitle, *An a-causal Connecting Principle.* Through his experience he came to believe that there are some happenings or incidences which are, to a large extent, meaningful and are not causally connected. Such happenings are very often called coincidences and always bring confusion. Jung was therefore very clever in distinguishing between them, and classified them as meaningful and meaningless.

But, first, the word coincidence; what does it mean? There was a house which was advertised in the Merseymart. It was in Harthill Avenue. I was interested in the house, but did not know where Harthill Avenue was. I checked in the A-Z and thought I knew where Harthill Avenue was, but I was confusing it with Harthill Road and went straight to Harthill Road. Unfortunately, that was a different place. I checked both sides of Harthill Road, but there was no sign of the Harthill Avenue house. As a consequence I went round in circles. I asked people around that area, but no one seemed to know where this Harthill Avenue was. I stopped and asked a certain man. He did not know either. A lady was driving behind me, and she knew the man could not help me. Later on, I decided to stop by the side of the road to check again in the A-Z. This lady who was driving behind me stopped too. She came out of her car and came to ask me what road I was looking for. I told her Harthill Avenue and to my amazement the lady said, "Oh, I was born in Harthill Avenue". This is what I would call a coincidence. I found it very remarkable and asked her name. She said 'Shirley Moss'. I told her I was going to include this coincidence in my book. I deliberately did this to make it more objective. *The Concise Oxford Dictionary* defines 'coincidence' as "notable occurrence of events or circumstances without apparent causal connection".

For example, in a dream I am told to go and catch an insect to use for medicine. If while relating the dream in the morning, that kind of insect, or a similar analogy, comes, it could be interpreted as a meaningful coincidence, and this is what Jung called synchronicity. Flew states "a pair or set, however remarkable, of occurrences cannot be said to be a coincidence or a series of coincidences if its members have some common causal origin; and that no pair or set of occurrences, however unconnected the circumstances which led up to them, can be correctly called a coincidence or a series of coincidences unless there is something remarkable about their coming together."[23]

Grattan-Guinness states that "The usual understanding of the concept of coincidence is that two or more events take place in some strikingly correlative way (for example, more or less simultaneously), but each event inhabits its own causative framework, disjointed from the framework of the other events."[24]

Jung, however, speaks of coincidence as a 'pointed' coincidence and of events in a synchronicity phenomenon as linked in a 'meaningful' manner, as if he were introducing a new species of coincidence. Thus, Flew argues that "To say that all (or some) coincidences are 'pointed' or 'meaningful' is to utter a tautology (or a ludicrous understatement): like saying all (or some) couples are married. Synchronicity is not a new species of coincidence, it is coincidence."[25] Flew adds, "To say that something is (just a) coincidence is not any sort of explanation: but is in part to deny the possibility of explanation."[26] Hence Jung, as Beloff, 1977, puts it, insisted that 'synchronicity' "postulates a meaning which is an a priori in relation to human consciousness and apparently exists outside man."[27]

Coincidences are also a form of precognition, just as dreams are. An example of such precognitions are given by Grattan-Guinness, in a review of a book, *What are Coincidences?* which I will address later. Jung also experienced some precognitive coincidences. In fact nearly everyone who has had such experiences could also claim that they are precognitive. It is these circumstances which lead me to say they overlap. Thus, in synchronicity, psychicism, telepathy and dreams there can be an element of precognition.

Jung believed that "synchronicity is a phenomenon that seems to be primarily connected with psychic conditions, that is to say with processes in the unconscious."[28] Its deepest strata, according to Jungian terminology, are formed by the "collective unconscious" potentially shared by all members of the race. The 'decisive factors' in the collective unconscious are archetypes which "constitute its structure". They were, as it were, the distilled memories of the human species, but cannot be represented in verbal terms, only in elusive symbols, which are shared by all mythologies.

They also provide 'patterns of behaviour' for all human beings in archetypal situations – confrontations with death, danger, love, conflict etc. In such situations the unconscious archetypes invade consciousness, carrying strong emotions and – owing perhaps to the archetype's indifference to physical space and time – facilitate the occurrence of 'synchronistic' events. The appearance of the scarab while a woman patient was telling Jung the dream she had of a scarab, and the bang which was heard in Freud's bookcase during Jung's visit to him, define what Jung meant by synchronicity: meaningful coincidences which, he maintained, ought to be distinguished from those which render no meaning. This brings us to the founders of seriality, synchronicity or coincidence.

Bibliography

1. Flew, A., *Readings in the Philosophical Problems of Parapsychology*, p. 67, Prometheus Books, New York, 1987.
2. Eysenck, H.J. et al., *Explaining the Unexplained*, p. 15, by BCA, London, N.Y., Toronto, 1982. *Mysteries of the Paranormal*, p. 15.
3. Flew, A. op. cit. p. 88.
4. Ibid p. 89.
5. Ibid p. 89.

6. Ibid p. 89-90.
7. Ibid p. 90.
8. Dunne, J.W., *An Experiment with Time*, p. 27, by A & C Black Ltd., London, 1927.
9. Flew, A., op. cit. p. 92.
10. Ibid p.92.
11. Dunne, op. cit. p. 27,
12. Morris, R.L., (1990) "The Challenge of Parapsychology", In A. Scot, *Frontiers of Science*, p. 51, Oxford: Basil Blackwell.
13. Ibid p. 51.
14. Ibid p. 51.
15. Ibid p. 51.
16. lbid p. 51.
17. lbid p. 52.
18. lbid p. 52.
19. lbid p. 52.
20. Flew, A., op. cit. p. 93.
21. lbid p. 104.
22. lbid p. 104.
23. Flew, A., *Journal of the Society for Psychical Research:* "Coincidences & Synchronicity" p. 198, vol. 37, no. 677.
24. Granton-Guinness, I., *Journal of the Society for Psychical Research*, p. 949, vol. 49, no. 778. *What are Coincidences?* Dec 1978.
25. Flew, A., *Journal of the Society for Psychical Research*, vol. 37, no. 677, Nov. 1953. *Coincidence & Synchronicity*, p. 199.
26. Ibid p. 199.
27. Beloff, J., *Psi Phenomena:* "Causal Versus Acausal Interpretation", p.574. *Journal of the Society for Psychical Research*, vol 49, no. 773, September 1977.
28. Koestler, A., *The Roots of Coincidence*, p. 95-96, Hutchinson & Co (Published) Ltd. London, 1972.

CHAPTER 3

Founders of Synchronicity

A s a young man in Orleans, Emile Deschamps was given a piece of plum pudding by Monsieur de Fortgibu. After ten years, he encountered another plum pudding in a restaurant in Paris. He asked for a portion; unfortunately it had already been ordered by Monsieur de Fortgibu. Interestingly, some years later he was invited to an event to eat a plum pudding and, eager to go, he accepted the invitation. While they were eating the pudding, he related the story of the earlier plum puddings to his friends and commented that what remained in the story was Monsieur de Fortgibu. Before he finished relating the story, the door opened and in walked Monsieur de Fortgibu. Monsieur de Fortgibu had been invited somewhere else, but did not have the correct address and had arrived at the house where Emile Deschamps was by mistake.

The above account is a fascinating kind of coincidence. The story has made a remarkable impression on many writers in the field of the paranormal. Some people could call this chance, but equally chance cannot continually keep on being repeated. At home in Malawi, we have a saying that "chance does not come twice" Ian Fleming in his *James Bond* said: "once is an accident, twice is a coincidence, three times is taking action". If something happens twice or more, the elderly say it is telling us something of a very important nature. Therefore I would assert that the story I have just related is not just mere chance. Emile Deschamps liked plum pudding very much. Thus, it seems to me, the Guardian Angel kept on directing him to places where there was plum pudding.

People of the past, especially in the eighteenth century, attributed coincidences to supernatural powers. The present writer holds the same view. These things do not just happen without reason. They are influenced by the gods. Thus Brian Inglis states that "Oedipus's encounter with his father was clearly predestined; Joseph's uncannily accurate interpretation of Pharaoh's dreams was made possible because the Lord had given him the power of divination; the portents accompanying Caesar's assassination were signals from the gods; when a witch's spell produced results, it was the devil's work."[1]

Later on the supernatural belief was superseded by belief in the laws of nature and this led to the development of rationalism. After rationalism, in the nineteenth century, came the belief in positivism which holds that every effect must have a cause.

Something Unknown to Science

Flammarion, to whom Monsieur Deschamps related the story of the plum pudding, recorded the tale in his *L'Inconnu* in 1900, and commented that "The little god chance sometimes produces extraordinary results."[2] Flammarion doubted whether coincidence and chance could be similar. Before that, in 1899, Alice Johnson, a Cambridge biologist, who also worked in the field of psychical research with Eleanor Sidgwick, pointed out that orthodox science should reconcile itself with the findings of telepathy. She wrote a book of about 60,000 words in which she defended the case that there was a cause. This was not in accordance with the orthodox scientists, who considered it pure superstition. However, Johnson still maintained that there was a cause which was not yet discovered by the scientists. Flammarion also came to the same view that what was known as chance must surely be something as yet unknown to science.

To this end, Flammarion related his own experience of his papers having been caught by the wind while writing a chapter on wind. A wind blew up and carried them into the trees. He did not bother to go and look for them; he just left the matter as it was, especially as it started raining shortly after the papers were carried up by the wind. Later, to his surprise, he received his notes already printed, without any single one of them being missing. What had happened was that the porter from the printing office who brought his proof-sheets found the papers in the rain and, frightened to think he had lost them himself, picked up the papers and gave them to the printing office without relating the story to anyone, with the result that the papers were in the end given to Flammarion.

Paul Kammerer

Kammerer was an Austrian biologist. He was impressed by *L'Inconnu*, Flammarion's work, and kept a log-book of coincidences from the age of twenty up to the age of forty. He recorded about one hundred coincidences in a more trivial way. "On November 4, 1910, his brother-in-law went to a concert where he had seat no. 9 and cloakroom ticket no. 9; the next day, at another concert, he had seat no. 21 and cloakroom ticket no. 21."[3] Kammerer did not hesitate in calling this a "series of the second order" on the basis that the same kind of coincidence occurred on two successive days.

Koestler related this to gamblers. He says: "It is indeed commonly believed that coincidences tend to come in series – gamblers have 'lucky days'."[4] For this reason, he called his book *Das Gesetz der Serie*. He defined a 'Serie' as "a lawful recurrence of the same or similar things and events – a recurrence or clustering, in time or space, whereby the individual members in the sequence, as far as can be ascertained by careful analysis – are not connected by the same active cause."[5] The phrase 'lawful recurrence' might seem to suggest that the series is governed by causal laws. Kammerer's view was opposite. He wanted to prove that "coincidences, whether they come singly or in series, are manifestations of a universal principle in nature which operates independently from physical causation."[6] In his view, "the laws of seriality were not yet explored." He believed in an a-causal principle which is active in the universe and tends to work towards unity.

He took the subject seriously, to the extent of going in the streets and parks, sitting on benches, counting the number of people who went in the same direction, distinguishing them by sex, age, dress, and if they carried umbrellas he would group them by colours, and he saw a typical clustering phenomenon which was familiar to statisticians, gamblers and insurance companies. Later, this data was subjected to careful statistical analysis in order to discover if certain of these parameters tended to cluster in time. However, Kammerer, being impressed, concluded as Koestler has shown in 1972.

"So far we have been concerned with the factual manifestations of recurrent series without attempting an explanation. We have found that recurrence of identical or similar data in contiguous areas of space or time is a simple empirical fact which cannot be explained by coincidence rule to such an extent that the concept of coincidence itself is negated."[7]

To this end Kammerer believed that there was in the universe an a-causal principle which works towards unity. Koestler in the *Act of Creation* also clarifies the same view.

There are two basic morphological archetypes, wrote Kepes, expression of order, coherence, discipline, stability on the one hand: expression of chaos, movement, vitality, change on the other. Common to the morphology of outer and inner processes, these are basic polarities recurring in physical phenomena, in the organic world and in human experience. They are 'the dynamic substance of our universe, written in every corner of nature.' ... Whenever we look, we find configurations that are either to be understood as patterns of order, of closure, of a tendency towards a centre, cohesion and balance, or as patterns of mobility, freedom. change, or opening. We recognise them in every visible pattern; we respond to their expression in nature's configurations and in human utterances, gestures, and acts. Cosmos and chaos ... the Apollonian spirit of measure and the Dionysian principle of chaotic life, organisation and randomness, stasis and kinesis.. all these are different aspects of the same polarity of configuration."[8] Koestler also adds "Thus the cliché about unity-in-variety represents one of the most powerful archetypes of human experience – cosmos arising out of chaos. We have seen it at work in the scientist's search for universal law; and when we see it reflected in a work of art, or in any corner of nature, however indirectly, we catch a faint echo of it."[9]

Seriality as A-causal Connection

However, with the story of Monsieur Deschamps, as stated earlier, Kammerer concluded that "seriality and its clusterings take place under the influence of a-causal connections rather than means of the familiarly caused pushes and pulls of physics."[10] Kammerer was also intrigued by the story narrated by his wife, who, in 1916, was reading a novel in which a certain Mrs Rohan appeared. "That day, while travelling on a streetcar, she saw a man who looked very like Prince Joseph Rohan and overheard him speaking of the village of Weissenbac. Later that day a shop assistant asked her if she happened to know of Weissenbac, as she had a delivery to make and did not know the correct postal address. That evening Prince Joseph Rohan paid the Kammerers a visit."[11] Kammerer's notebook was packed with examples of such things, which went beyond mere chance and pointed to a universal principle of seriality.

Kammerer's work was so impressive that it was regarded by Einstein, a famous scientist, as original. But Peat, an American writer, in his book, *Synchronicity* (1988), suggests that Kammerer's ideas on chance clusterings are not well known today, and scientists are not impressed by his work. The problem is that whilst Kammerer believed that patterns of nature manifest themselves in patterns of chance, "there is a major logical drawback in accepting his evidence that serial clusterings are somehow different from purely random ones."[12]

Peat gives an example of "the tossing of a coin. On average there will be as many heads as there are tails but in any long sequence of tosses there may appear to be a run of heads; for example, three, four or even five heads in succession."[13] Peat adds that "If a particular run of heads were to persist or to occur repeatedly, a sceptical gambler would suspect that the coin used was not true."[14]

Loopholes in Seriality

Peat sees some loopholes in Kammerer's theory of seriality. For example, "in analysing clusterings, such as a sequence in coin tosses or the coincidence of several people wearing green hats on a bus, the problem is one of differentiating between a mysterious underlying affinity and the result of pure chance."[15] Also, "When one leaves coin tossings and roulette wheels for the coincidence of names, places, and the way people are dressed, there is the additional difficulty of determining what is a normal probability and how much a given sequence deviated from it."[16] Jung was then clever enough to point out that what distinguishes synchronicity from ordinary coincidence rests on its 'meaningful' coincidence.

Carl Jung

It is believed by some writers in the field of parapsychology that Jung's theory on synchronicity' originated from Kammerer's principle of 'seriality'. Jung examined the principle of seriality and regarded it as mere or meaningless coincidence. As Brian Inglis puts it, in his book *'Coincidence' A Matter of Chance – or Synchronicity?* (1990), Kammerer's ideas attracted the interest of Jung. For a time, Jung was even tempted to accept that 'clusters' lay outside conventional causality. While he was engaged on research into the history of the classical 'fish' symbol (Pisces), fish cropped up in his life six times in twenty-four hours, a run which for him seemed to have "a certain 'numinous quality".[17] This fish coincidence will be explored further in chapter 4. Jung was fascinated but in the end dismissed it and felt there was "no real justification for regarding it as anything but fortuitous".[18]

Needless to say, Jung became interested in another principle. While he was doing his research on the collective unconscious, he came across a number of coincidences, so meaningfully connected that their chance occurrence would represent a degree of improbability that would have to be expressed by an astronomically large figure. He believed them to be connected to another principle, which is ascertained as contingency of events, to which he regarded the principle of 'synchronicity' as belonging. For example the arrival of a golden scarab in time was purely what Jung would call a meaningful coincidence. To this end, he coined his synchronicity theory as 'meaningful' and seriality' as meaningless. Inglis commented that "If meaningless coincidences are frequent, there must occasionally occur coincidences that have meaning".[19] The philosopher Herbert Spencer wrote, as Inglis puts it, "coincidences of which the elements are related in some significant way."[20]

Inglis, however, thinks Spencer was imbued with the rise of positivism – or materialism. He was of the opinion that meaningful coincidences came out of chance, not through the gods. Hence the materialistic reliance on the principle of causality that everything happens for a reason or must have a cause was challenged. When Jung wrote his essay on synchronicity in 1952, he gave it a sub-title: *An Acausal Connecting Principle*. Pauli also wrote on the concept of synchronicity. These two worked in collaboration, but Jung himself was first.

Successful Meeting of Freud and Jung

Jung was born in the Swiss village of Keswill in 1875. He had been fascinated by dreams since he was a young boy. He specialised in psychiatry and started corresponding with

Professor Sigmund Freud, who was also interested in the interpretation of dreams. Freud was working at Burgholzi clinic, and these two met in 1907. Their discussion, as Peat puts it, was regarded as an unqualified success; "Jung admitted to a 'religious' crush with undeniable erotic overtones", and Freud, for his part, treated the younger man as his adopted son and wrote, "I could hope for no one better than yourself to continue and complete my work."[21]

Jung very soon rose to power. In 1908, at the first international gathering in Salzburg, he was elected president of the psycho-analytic congress. Although Freud and Jung were very close, they had some differences. Freud's beliefs were in a rational, scientific tradition; Jung was more interested in spiritualism, fantasy, and the curious nature of images drawn and dreamed by his patients. Freud was very worried about Jung's belief in spiritualism, and warned him against being overwhelmed by occultism. However, during Jung's first visit to Vienna, the two psychologists heard a bang from Freud's bookcase; Jung used this to elaborate his theory of synchronicity. As Peat puts it, "Jung experienced a red-hot sensation in his diaphragm, and at the same time the two men heard a loud crack from the direction of the bookcase. Jung suggested this was an example of "catalytic exteriorization," to which Freud replied, "sheer bosh". The younger man predicted that a second event would occur, and sure enough, another report was heard, the sound of which shook Freud considerably.[22] Jung just said this and confessed that he did not know what made him believe the bang was going to be repeated.

Although Freud did not agree with Jung on the synchronistic theory, he did, at a later stage, believe in the principle. Thus Freud wrote to Jung in 1912 explaining a similar kind of experience, but regarded it as a slip of the tongue. Jung responded to Freud's letter by saying "You see, my dear Professor, as long as you hand out this stuff, I don't give a damn for your symptomatic action; they shrink to nothing in comparison with the formidable beam in my brother Freud's eyes.[23]

Jung, however, resigned as President of the Psycho-analytic

Congress, which pleased Freud, who wrote, as Peat has indicated, "So we are at last rid of the brutal, sanctimonious Jung".[24] Jung was then free to develop the ideas of synchronicity without anyone disturbing him. He argued, in his psychological research, that "Each person is the result of a balance between the forces of intuition, sensation, thinking, and feeling. Sometimes it is difficult to come to terms with other people's thinking. We always take what someone is doing as wrong if we don't approve of it. In the end one decides to go one's own way. My cousin, who is also a friend, always argues with me about what I am writing. She takes dreams as the act of the devil, as does another friend, who also holds the same view. They argue against my belief that dreams and meaningful coincidences come from God. It's a belief which no one can take from me because of my own experiences, and I am convinced that there must be a guardian angel. What we know is what we apprehend by our intuition. Some might argue that intuition is subjective. While this is true, intuition can in most cases be stronger than science. Science is based on probability and can fail to predict the future.

I wonder how on earth people could believe dreams are from the devil when it is through dreams that Joseph was saved. It was God who inverted Pharaoh's dream with an idea of saving Joseph. So Pharaoh's dream coincided with Joseph's imprisonment. In that case it was a meaningful coincidence, 'Synchronicity', as Jung might call it. Equally it is true to say that in everything there is a profane and a sacred facet.

Strange Images Appearing to Jung

In reading Jung's book on *Memories, Dreams and Reflection*, one sees that Jung went deeper and deeper in his thinking. In one of his dreams he metaphorically regarded his mind as a house which had a hidden basement, and had a trap door leading to a remote 'prehistoric cavern.' He was more and more discovering a universal mind, which he later called the collective or objective unconscious. He believed this was common to all the human race. He conversed with both internal and independent figures, including Philemon, the wise old man, and Anima, the young woman, who had once served as a spiritual guide to Simon-Magnus, Lao-tzu, and Klingsor. With regard to the wise old man, Jung wrote, as Peat asserts, "... at times he seemed to me quite real, as if he were a living personality. I went walking up and down the garden with him, and to me he was what the Indians call a guru. He said things which I had not consciously thought. For I observed clearly that it was he who spoke, not I."[25]

These images reached their climax when, in 1916, Jung's whole house was haunted. It was on a Sunday morning and Jung's household did not even hear someone ring the doorbell. "The atmosphere was thick, believe you me, then I knew that something had to happen. The whole house was filled as if there were a crowd present, crammed full with spirits. They were packed deep right up to the door, and the air was so thick it was scarcely possible to breathe. As for myself I was all a-quiver with the question: 'For God's sake, what in the world is this?' Then they cried out in chorus, ' We have come from Jerusalem where we found not what we sought.' "[26]

Whilst possessed with these spirits, Jung wrote the *Seven Sermons to the Dead (vii Sermons ad Mortuos)*. He wrote this in a more prophetic way. The book itself, as Peat states, "becomes a metaphor for the emergence of consciousness out of the collective unconscious and ultimately from the psychoid which is prior to the distinction between matter and mind."[27] Jung then postulated an account for the origin of mind just as modern physics postulates a theory that the world was created by the primordial big bang. Jung's theory suggests that "The human mind can be excavated far beyond the personal unconscious, and in its deepest levels, it possesses a rich structure of dynamic forces, symmetrical patterns, and autonomous centres of energy."[28] Jung gave a background of how matter and mind came into being. If his theory is examined critically, one sees similarities with that of Kammerer, as he compared it to an "umbilical cord uniting with thought, feelings, science and art with the womb of the universe which gave birth to them."[29] There is in both theories involvement with nature.

Wolfgang Pauli

Pauli was born in 1900 in Vienna, where his father was a professor of biochemistry at the University. He joined the University of Munich at the age of eighteen, where Werner Heisenberg met him and was informed by Sommerfield, one of the lecturers, that Pauli was one of his best students. Since that time Pauli and Heisenberg were friends, and worked together. Heisenberg wrote about the new quantum mechanics and Pauli later wrote about the same thing. Pauli propounded a theory of the hydrogen atom that "convinced most physicists that quantum media mechanics is correct." Pauli also wrote about the 'exclusion principle', which was a continuation of Heisenberg's quantum mechanics theory, ('Uncertainty theory'). This contributed to the notion of synchronicity, which Jung defined as an "a-causal connecting principle". This is exactly what Pauli propounded in his theory of exclusion, when he argued that, at the quantum level, "all nature engages in an abstract dance".[30]

Pauli co-operated with Jung on the subject of synchronicity. He accepted Jung's view that "meaningful coincidences are a manifestation of an a-causal, (i.e.; extraphysical) principle "equal in importance to physical causality". But Pauli called it a 'metaphysical' or 'absolute order' of the cosmos which provides the background of physical phenomena, as Jung's archetypes of the collective unconscious provide the substratum of consciousness (and are thus, by definition, beyond its grasp).

A very interesting thing happened to Professor J. Franck, a colleague of Pauli, in his laboratory in Göttingen. Early one afternoon, as Koestler et al. put it in *Coincidence*, a complicated apparatus for the study of atomic phenomena collapsed without apparent cause. Frank wrote about this to Pauli at his Zurich address and, after some delay, received an answer in an envelope with a Danish stamp. Pauli wrote that he had gone to visit Bohr (in Copenhagen) and at the actual time of the mishap was in Franck's Göttingen railroad station.

It is hard for some to believe the account given above, but easy for some of us who have experienced similar coincidences. It is this account which made Pauli agree with Jung about the principle of synchronicity. Pauli's life seemed to be dominated with incidents like the one given above, to the extent that his colleagues thought them worthy of a scientific name and called them the 'Pauli Effect'.

Pauli made a tremendous contribution to physics. As Peat has commented, "the underlying pattern of the whole dance has a profound effect on the behaviour of each individual particle".[31] It is, as Peat asserts, "The exclusion principle which causes electrons in an atom to stack up a series of energy levels and makes one atom chemically distinguishable from another."[32] Peat goes on to say, "It is the Pauli principle which gives rise to the rich chemistry of nature; without it, the whole universe would seem more or less featureless. It is the symmetric dance of the Pauli principle which is at work behind the intense coherent light of the laser as well as superfluids and superconduction."[33]

Looking at the three main pioneers of synchronicity, Kammerer, Pauli, and Jung, it seems as if Jung used both Kammerer and Pauli to propound his theory of synchronicity. Having examined seriality, he dismissed it by regarding it as meaningless; even so, seriality gave him a foundation on which he based his theory of synchronicity and regarded it as meaningful. Hence, it is right to say that both Kammerer and Jung formulated the theory of synchronicity, in the sense that they both believed in an a-casual principle. On the other hand, Jung worked in collaboration with Pauli. Thus the theory of synchronicity seems to originate both from physics through Pauli and psychology through Carl Jung. For this reason Koestler calls synchronicity 'The Jung-Pauli Theory'. Kammerer is regarded as their precursor, someone who gave them guidance. Unfortunately, Kammerer died young, at the age of forty-five, when he committed suicide after someone tampered with his experiments. But there are still many writers today who are fascinated with the theory of seriality. The Queen stated in her 1993 Christmas message to the nation that writing books is an ideal way of communicating with the future generation. To this end Kammerer has influenced some of us with his doctrine of seriality.

Bibliography

1. Inglis, B., *Coincidence: A Matter Of Chance – Or Synchronicity*, p.2, Hutchinson, London, 1990,
2. Ibid p. 1-2,
3. Koestler, A.; *The Roots of Coincidence*, p. 84, Hutchinson, London, 1972.
4. Ibid p. 84.
5. Ibid p. 85.
6. Ibid p. 85.
7. Ibid p. 86.
8. Koestler, A., *The Act of Creation*, p. 389, Hutchinson of London, 1964/5.
9. Ibid p. 390.
10. Peat, F. D., *Synchronicity*, p. 8. Bantam Books, USA, 1987.
11. Ibid p. 7-9.
12. Ibid p. 9.
13. Ibid p. 9.
14. Ibid p. 9.
15. Ibid p. 9.
16. Ibid p. 9-10.
17. Inglis, B., op. cit p. 4.
18. Ibid p. 4.
19. Ibid p. 5.
20. Ibid p. 5.
21. Ibid, F.D., op. cit p. 11.
22. Ibid p. 11.
23. Ibid p. 11.
24. Ibid p. 12.

25. Ibid p. 12.
26. Ibid p. 13.
27. Ibid p. 13.
28. Ibid p. 14.
29. Ibid p. 14.
30. Ibid p. 16.
31. Ibid p. 16.
32. Ibid p. 16.
33. Ibid p. 16.

CHAPTER 4

Seriality

Paul Kammerer was the founder of seriality and his aim was to prove that coincidences, "whether they come singly or in series, are manifestations of a universal principle in nature which operates independently from physical causation."[1] These laws, he maintained, were similar to those of physics, although he agreed that those of seriality are still unexplored.

Coincidence and Physics

Kammerer tried to equate coincidence with physics, but had no support from other science experts of his day. The argument was that synchronicity is about paranormal happenings in the universe in which two unrelated events tend to coincide. Such happenings seemed to some as not to equate with physics, which sees the cosmos, as Allan Combs et al. put it, "as a loose assemblage of objects, forces, and energy."

At the dawn of the twentieth century, physics had its foundation through imagination. The atoms were regarded as the basis of the physical world. The atomic theory had to do with Descartes' geometry, which was viewed as a three-dimensional space. Within a few years this belief was shaken. The atoms were then dissolved into abstractions and were now regarded as probabilities written on the walls of mathematicians. This was superseded by the two theories (i) Einstein's general theory of relativity and (ii) Quantum theory. These two theories saw the universe as an undivided field, wherein atoms and stars were seen as properties of this field. They were compared to vortices in water. Whilst these vortices may interact with each other and cancel each other out, their origin is not separate, but that is how they are viewed.

In contrast, quantum theory does not deal with the existence of objects; it deals with events. Separate entities have no room for quantum theory, but events. These events are all inter-connected. To this end, many subatomic particles are not treated as separate in the theory. The particles are treated as one totality in the system or as a whole. The quantum theory sees each particle as part of a larger unity. David Bohin maintained that the universe or the whole cosmos should be perceived as one, not divided. The theory of synchronicity then emphasises the same wholeness as in physics. Events are seen in the meaningful way that to this end the two events are related and wholly joined together. These two meaningful events may differ in time and space, but still refer to one thing in a meaningful way.

The quantum theory was propounded by Einstein, and was interpreted by Bohr and Heisenberg. Heisenberg, in his equation, discovered that the amount of information obtained in the particular atomic particle in one way or another is limited. For example, the position of a particle can be measured in time with much accuracy but in the end the velocity of the particle will be unidentified.

From the above it can be deduced that the more some scientists and psychologists undermine the paranormal phenomena, the more it can also be argued that other fields have loopholes as well, as has already been shown in physics. This applies to psychology as well. For example, the orthodox do recognise the limitations and shortcomings of Pavlov's experiments, as Koestler has stated in his book, *The Ghost in the Machine*. Thus he asserts, "The dog on the laboratory table, predictably salivating at the sound of a gong, has become a paradigm of existence, a kind of anti-Promethean myth, and the word conditioning with its rigid deterministic connotations, has become a key formula for explaining why we are what we are, and for explaining away moral responsibility."[2]

Before the First World War broke out, Prof. John Broadus Watson of John Hopkins University in Baltimore proclaimed that "the time has come when psychology must discard all reference to consciousness. Its sole task is the prediction and control of behaviour, and introspection can form no part of its method."[3] By that he meant activities which are observable; these can be compared to 'public events' in physics. He declared that mental events are private events which are subjective in a sense, and that they can "only be made public through statements based on introspection." They have to be excluded from the domain of science."[4]

Through the teaching above, the Behaviourists proceeded to purge psychology of all intangibles and unapproachables. Therefore terms such as 'consciousness', 'mind', 'imagination', and 'purpose', together with a score of others, were declared to be unscientific, treated as dirty words, and banned from the vocabulary. Watson did not want science to include the words which are subjective, i.e. sensation, perception, image, desire, purpose and thinking. To some extent Watson rejected the idea of consciousness and mind. Professor Skinner of Harvard University, the neo-Behaviourist, followed Watson. He stated in his work, *Science and Human Behaviour* that 'mind' and ideas' are non-existent entities. Equally, since mental or psychic events are asserted to lack the dimensions of physical science, there is every reason for rejecting them.

My contention is that if some see paranormal phenomena as insufficient in the sense that they are subjective, it could be argued that nearly every field is insufficient, as we have shown above. There are, in every discipline, some hidden things, just as there are some hidden thoughts – Freud's slip of the tongue. Yet again, unlike other fields, psi-phenomena are distinguished from the other fields since they are from God and therefore difficult to understand. These things are very puzzling and are very deep in themselves. Since they are puzzling, they will continue to happen in a mysterious way.

No matter how small and simple they may be, I still take note of them. For example, I could be reading a book in the library and when I come home to rest and turn the television on, the first item to appear could be what I had been reading. It would puzzle me less if I were reading the newspaper and what I was reading appeared on the television, because it could be argued that it was the issue of the day or of the week, because what is on the television is normally a repetition of what is in the newspapers. Since this is my day-to-day life, these coincidences were, at first, hardly meaningful to me, but I have yet another one of the same sort which I have taken to be meaningful.

I don't normally listen to the radio in the morning as I am fond of television. It is only in the morning that I listen to Radio Four or Radio Merseyside. This particular day, Saturday, 20th November, 1993, I went to the library as usual, then went home. I was so tired that I did not want to strain my eyes watching the television, so I turned on the radio. I was listening to Radio Four and the first thing I heard was a debate about parapsychology with Dr. Morris, Chair of Parapsychology at Edinburgh University. Honestly I was puzzled. I had spent the morning reading about parapsychology in the library and I switched on Radio Four for the first time in the afternoon to find them talking about exactly the same thing on the radio, the very day I was trying to define parapsychology. I polished my definition through hearing Dr. Morris. Sometimes I find it more useful to hear someone talking than reading from a book.

Whilst on the train to London, l met Dr. Veronica Moss, Medical Director, who was at that moment working in London. She had come to Liverpool for a talk. However, talking on the same subject, she said sometimes she has something in mind which she wants to say and finds that someone had already mentioned it in the exact manner. I categorised this as in the line of telepathy. Inglis related a story in his book, *Coincidence: A Matter of Chance – Or Synchronicity?* which was told by Alice Johnson, to whom I have already referred in the previous chapter. Alice Johnson cited the case that the Homer Scholar, Walter Leaf, had sent to her while she was at Cambridge in 1871. Leaf had two teeth which had been knocked out while playing cricket. "I had a good deal of pain, which gave me such a restless night that I was glad, contrary to my usual habit, to get up early next morning and go to early chapel. In the Psalms for the morning (lviii, 6) came the verse, "Break their teeth, O God, in their mouths!"[5]

Paranormal Phenomena As Public Events

A similar story is related by Koestler in the book, *The Challenge of Chance*. He tells of a story witnessed by four people: "In June, 1961 my wife and I moved into a house we had built as a summer residence in the mountain village of Alpbach, in the Austrian Tyrol. Alpbach is a place with a strong Catholic tradition, and though we are not Catholics, we agreed to have the house blessed by the parish priest, Herr Pfarrer Danninger, to comply with local custom. On the morning of Sunday, June 25th, the day appointed for the ceremony, while waiting for Pfarrer Danninger, I was reading André Maurois' biography of Alexander Fleming. It contains a passage in which Maurois discusses the hypothesis that the biblical hyssop, which the ancient Hebrews used in their purification rites during the harvest feast, was a plant which carried the mould penicillium; and he quotes verse 7 from Psalm 51: 'Purge me with hyssop and I shall be clean.' When I got to this passage my wife called, 'The Herr Pfarrer is here'; so I put a book mark in that page and went downstairs. Our neighbours, the farmer Othmar Redinger and his wife, joined in and after the traditional glasses of schnapps, Pfarrer Danninger performed the ceremony, which culminated in his sprinkling the walls with holy water and reading out, in German, Ps. 51, v.7 'Purge me with hyssop and I shall be clean.' "[6]

At first I did not really have any intention of writing on seriality, because although these things happen, they did not really mean anything to me. But I eventually met Dr. Vincent Arkley, who has innumerable instances to relate, and these have left a tremendous impression on him. Dr. Arkley is a retired lecturer in chemistry, and believes that the laws of chance rest on experience. As such they cannot be challenged, because whoever has experienced them cannot give up. He can defend them. His brother always argues with him, wondering why a scientist, as he is, should waste time on these things. Although his brother argues like that, one day he himself had a lucid dream. One afternoon he was relating the story to Dr. Arkley. By then they had just parked the brother's car. His car was stolen in this dream. A few hours later, two boys tried to steal his car. Fortunately, they were caught quickly.

Thus it seems that in everything there is an element of premonition. Some people seem to 'know beforehand what is going to happen. There is in everything the idea of *déjà vu*: a feeling that something has happened before. Nietsche the German philosopher, declared, "There is not such a thing as an original idea. What we say must have already been said by someone else to a certain extent. Solomon writes on the very same thing in Ecclesiastes, "What has been is what will be, and what has been done is what will be done; and there is nothing new under the sun. Is there a thing of which it said, 'See, this is new'? It has been already, in the ages before us."[7]

It seems as if the number 23 has some significance or special quality. Dr. Vincent Arkley told me the number is always repeated in his family. If a wife or a husband was born on 23rd, one of the children would also be born on 23rd. It also happens that if you were born on 23rd of any month, your wedding will also be on the same date, not necessarily chosen deliberately, but just happening. Dr. Brian Inglis related a similar story, in which a couple who were getting married bought a wedding ring, and later found that 'A23P' was engraved on it. The girl's name was Ann and the boy's name was Peter and they were getting married on 23rd. Freud too believed in twenty-three and twenty-seven day cycles that combine to affect behaviour. Kammerer believed that clusters of recurrent events propagate in cyclic fashion, like waves of water. Only the peaks of the waves are visible; the

76

troughs are hidden from view. He compared this to the old theories of periodicity which included the "Pythagorean symbolic use of the number seven. The seven musical notes in an octave do repeat." He also reviewed Goethe's revolving good and bad days, and Freud's belief in twenty-three and twenty-seven day cycles that combine to affect behaviour, as has already been stated above. Kammerer, being a biologist, concluded that cyclic behaviour was characteristic of natural processes in general.

I took my niece to Lee Manor College in Knowsley, Liverpool, where she was starting a course in Health Care. I stayed a few hours because she started college late after her friends had already enrolled. The day she started was the 27th September. At home in Malawi we don't normally celebrate birthdays except for a few. For this reason I did not take any note of my niece's birthday. She had just come from home so I did not really know when she was born. It is difficult to know when there are many nieces in the family. However, while in class, my niece was asked to write about herself, her name, date of birth and where she came from. Her tutor was sitting next to her and I was on the other side. She wrote her date of birth as the 27th September. To my amazement, her tutor exclaimed: "Oh, is it your birthday today? You were born on the 27th September and you are starting on the 27th September." She saw something very unusual in this. I was by then writing this chapter on seriality, but even so I was not as impressed as all that. I took it as just a coincidence, not really something to think about. Perhaps there was something significant, because her friends started one week earlier than the 27th September. My niece came late from Malawi. So she happened to start on her birthday.

Tan Donald, as Inglis states in his book, *Coincidence, A Matter of Chance – Or Synchronicity?*, while travelling on a train from Edinburgh to the south, met someone whom he had never met before. They agreed to have lunch together, and sat at a table where there was an Indian couple. Donald said, as reported, by Inglis, "I felt very much at ease sitting beside this gracious and handsome Hindu lady, beautifully attired in her sari and expensively jewelled. I asked her which part of India she came from. She replied that she came from Calcutta, where I had lived, and I told her I had been billeted in a large dwelling house in Carrington Street. She was dumbfounded momentarily, but recomposed herself to tell me that she used to live there as a child. Then with some urgency she asked if I remembered the number of the house. 'Number Seven', I replied, not daring to expect that this could possibly have been her house. Imagine the amazement and thrill we both felt when we realised that it was the house that had at one time belonged to her father." [8]

To say that the above account was a mere chance would not be acceptable to Donald. To him, the meeting of the man in the train and the arrangement of the lunch together and the meeting of the lady were significant. It is in this sense that the principle of seriality could also be regarded as meaningful.

Arkley told me another story with which he was also impressed. His brother in law and his wife came for a visit from Canada, and they all went sight-seeing to Albert Docks in Liverpool. As they were entering one of the gates, they bumped into an old friend of his brother-in-law, with whom he had been at school and college. Arkley was fascinated. He was amazed as to why the two of them should decide to go to the dock on that day and at exactly the same time.

When Arkley told me all his experiences on seriality, I said to him that it seems as if there is God or a guardian angel behind them. He commented that he would rather use 'collective unconscious' in the same way as Jung did, Arkley, however, told me that often when he wants to ring someone and he goes to the telephone, as he is about to pick it up the person he was trying to ring rings him first. He has a friend in Canada, and if he thinks of ringing him, the friend rings at the same time and it has been like that all through. The very same thing happened to me. I had taken Arkley's phone number to work in a notebook. On 3rd December 1993 I took the notebook home to ring him. I told my niece I was going to ring him round about 9 p.m. I was asking my niece to lower the volume of the television, so that I could ring him to ask when I could take my work to him; he rang me before I had finished telling my niece. He told me to bring my work to him in a week's time.

This often happens to me in the office. When I am looking for somebody's number, that person rings me first. The other day I was going to ring a colleague, Moira Rangel, Deputy Divisional Social Work Manager. Just as I picked up the phone, she was there ringing me. The story does not end there. After I had put the receiver down, I rushed to the bank, and was surprised to meet her sister, whom I had not seen for a long time. I told her I was talking to her sister. I must admit I found something in this. I had not met Moira's sister for almost two years or more. I could not even remember when I last saw her. It might have been more than two years. To meet her after talking to her sister seems to imply something to me.

Animal Precognition

Animals can also give us an indication of what is going to happen to us. This precognition in animals happens almost in the same way as in a dream. Dreams tell us what is ahead of us. Almost always in the African continent animals can indicate something. Supposing one member of the village is sick and an owl alights on the roof of that sick person's house, the elderly would say that he or she will not escape death. Certainly that person will die the same night or the following day. A colleague from Uganda, Sister Mary Nakku, who was at that time studying at John Moore's University, lost a sister in 1993. The evening before her sister died, she was sitting by the window watching the television when all of a sudden an owl came. She did not know what it meant. The following day her sister died.

There is also the issue of the dog if it wags its tail. The elderly say the dog is doing it for a reason. Something is going to happen and it does. My mother, who was born in 1901 and died in 1993, told me yet another story. When she got married she went to stay at my father's place, which is unusual, because at home in my area it is the man who goes to live at the wife's place. However, her sister was seriously sick, and some people from my mother's home came to tell her. It was late when my mother got the message but she still had to go that same evening. Some women and men from my father's place accompanied her. They had to walk a distance of 26 miles. It was round about three or four a.m. when they were about to reach my mother's place. Something appeared in front of them in the form of a human being – very tall. It could also be called a ghost. It went rolling, rolling in front of them, and would leave them for a distance and stop, then lean on a tree. It would start again, coming back towards them, and stop. Later on it disappeared. With that they all agreed that the sister had definitely died; they would not find her alive, and so it turned out.

In the account given above, it seems to me that in everything there is an element of precognition. Even in small, small things which happen to us there is something which precedes the event. Dr. Keith Hearne asserts that "If premonitions are genuine, then they imply, perhaps, at first sight, that everything is pre-planned and that they portray events lined up and ready to happen. We can occasionally foresee those events, but they are quite inevitable."[9] Perhaps it is right to mention that the theory of pre-planning is to some extent misleading, because this equates to the theory of predestination. But I take premonition as in the range of God's providence. As I stated, I was at first not impressed with seriality, but things started happening to me one after another. Although I could hardly see the meaning in some of them, I am persuaded that they are indeed as meaningful as synchronistic ones. They tell us something referring to the future or pointing to the future. Although we may not see it at that particular time, it gives us an insight. When it happens, we see what synchronicity was referring to or pointing at.

Unconscious versus Conscious

At the end of August, 1993, one Saturday, I was with a colleague of mine who is a hairdresser. I went to her house. It was late and just after she closed her shop,and I was so lonely that I went with her to Bootle. While we were at her house, we spoke of going to London specifically to buy fish from Africa. We could not stop commenting on the fish. At 8.30 p.m. I started going back to my house in Liverpool and when I reached the door I found a parcel and a letter. I could tell from the handwriting that it was from my brother. I entered the house and opened the parcel. Sure enough, it was fish. My sister-in-law had sent three big fish from Africa.

It seems to me that when we mention something, it is already there or on its way. I went home to Malawi in 1993. Having no money, I decided to borrow some from the Lombard Bank. In my section at work, Adult Care Planning, we live as a family; everything one wants to do has to be debated first. I would not be wrong to say that there is a spirit of humanity.

However, on this occasion I wanted to borrow money and everyone in the section knew I had applied and had been accepted. Sandra Edwards, a week after I had received their approval, asked me whether the Lombard Bank had sent the cheque and I replied that they had not. She went on to say, "But it has taken a long time, and I said "Yes", and went on to say I did not think they were going to give me the money. It was during the lunch hour when Sandra asked me, and in the morning I had already checked the post before I went to work. It was round about one o'clock when Sandra asked me. So they all comforted me. Nargis Anwar said, "A solution will be found; you will get the money from somewhere." As it was, I finished work and went home round about six p.m. I checked the post and there was the cheque. I was anxious to go to work in the morning to tell them I had received the cheque. The second mail comes at one p.m. It follows then that the time Sandra was asking about the cheque coincided with the delivery of the cheque. Although I have put this in this chapter, I think it has much more to do with synchronicity: things happening at the same time as if there was an a-causal reason. I have associated this with the theory of a guardian angel. This is to some extent natural, the way God arranged things to be.

Not Coincidence but Nature

I regard it as nature, because it seems to me that when you mention something in desperation, a miracle happens. A white man in South Africa, John Botha from the Transvaal town of Nelspruit, said he was on his knees saying his prayers before going to bed when he thought to ask the question, "What is it, God, that you want from us in South Africa?" Suddenly, according to Colonel Botha, an angel, brilliant and glowing, appeared before him and said, "I want the whole nation on its knees for one day."[10] The angel, then, came at the exact time when the Colonel mentioned God. For this reason I am inclined to say these are not coincidences, they are more than coincidences; they are part of nature. Thus Jung was prepared to say, "Natural laws are statistical truths, which means that they are completely valid only when we are dealing with macrophysical quantities". Although "In the realm of very small quantities (sub-atomic scale) prediction becomes uncertain if not impossible, because very small quantities no longer behave in accordance with the known natural laws".[11]

Chance, however, as Jung observed, seems to be meaningless, and to fall as a general rule within the limits of probability."[12] For example, Jung gives another instance of synchronicity concerned with fish. April 1 is referred to as April fish in most European countries. Jung happened to be working on the fish symbol. This was on 1st April, 1949, which was a Friday. Jung's family had fish for lunch. Incidentally, someone happened to mention the custom involved in making an 'April Fish'. Also when his patient arrived, as Peat states, "Jung was shown a picture of a fish and a piece of embroidery with a fish on it. On the following day another patient told him of a dream of a large fish that had occurred the night before. While writing down these accounts, Jung went for a walk beside the lake and saw a large fish".[13] Peat adds that "Jung himself gives prominence to this pattern of fishy occurrences. But to many readers they will seem to be nothing more than simple coincidences."[14] Jung confessed that none of the people who related the stories of fish knew anything about this study except for one person.

One could be inclined to believe that there were some sort of supernatural powers involved just to help Jung in his study. Jung then asserts that "It is, admittedly, exceedingly odd that the fish theme recurs no less than six times within twenty-four hours."[15] He also adds, "One must remember that fish on Friday is the usual thing, and on April 1 one might easily think of the April fish."[16] While this is true, why should he meet those patients on that particular day, not any other day of the week? The issue at stake is not so much the Friday, but those people. Why did they come forward on the same day, not a Tuesday or Wednesday, although he had not seen some of them for years? I think it is so much to do with the fish symbol study he was undertaking, although such incidents can give a valid meaning in some rare cases, there are still some chances which do not show any causality. Jung then stated, "Since we have an inveterate conviction of the absolute validity of causal law, we regard this explanation of chance as being adequate. But if the causal principle is only relatively valid, then it follows, even though in the vast majority of cases an apparently chance series can be causally experienced."[17]

Peat, however, asserts that the above account is confirmed by the research of a Swiss analyst, Arnold Mindel. Mindel began his professional training as a physicist but later switched to Jungian psychology, which he studied in Zurich. His interest in synchronicity and the possibility of resonances between physics and psychology led him to conduct a survey by means of a questionnaire sent out to a number of Jungians.[18]

Mindel's work, together with Jung's work and that of other commentators, shows that "It is possible to build up a profile for synchronistic happenings."[19] Jung also pointed out, as Peat puts it, "It is the nature of synchronicity to have meaning and, in particular, to be associated with a profound activation of energy deep within the psyche."[20]

Small puzzling Coincidences

I was thrilled, one particular week, when I was going to London to buy an air ticket for my niece who was coming over to England. It was on a Friday, and I was driving from the Social Services building across the flyover, when I saw Mr. John Hamilton, a retired councillor of Liverpool City Council. Though retired, he is still very active in the community, and is a member of the Executive of Merseyside Racial Equality Council (MREC). He is very respectable and a man of integrity, always willing to help in time of crisis. He was going to the trade union building, and when I sounded the horn he saw me. The following morning I met him again when I was travelling to London. I was impressed, and noted it in my diary. Apart from seeing him at MREC executive meetings, I have never just met him outside. Yet on this particular Friday I met him and again on the following Saturday, travelling together to London. It is difficult for me to call it mere chance. As both Jung and Rudolf Otto put it, this sort of coincidence carries the numinous quality. It is something inexpressible, or 'something there' in its simplest form.

It was also on a particular Sunday in June that I went to visit an old friend of mine. She had invited me to come on Sunday, but, as it happened, I did not find her. Someone from her country, Bangladesh, had invited her to visit them about something urgent, so she had to go there. When I reached her house, I met her daughter, whom I had not seen for years. She too was just coming to visit her mum. She is married with two children; she too did not know that the mother was not in. She was excited to see me and insisted I stay to have a chat with her but I was in a hurry so I had to leave. On my way home I met my friend's children, whom I referred to in *The Usefulness Of Dreams*, and they were going to town. I decided to give them a lift and, upon reaching the town, the first person I saw was the husband of the girl I had left at my friend's house. By then I had already told the children about this girl I met at my friend's house. Then later it was her husband. I had not seen the husband for years. I saw the husband after I had just finished telling the girl's story, and there was the husband. I pointed out the man to the children. One of the kids commented that it was a coincidence and I said, "Yes, Seriality." The children knew I was writing a book on synchronicity.

Some time in June I went to Professor Bradshaw to give him my manuscript to check the English. I had nothing in my fridge except one tomato and cucumber and perhaps milk. Before I left I was considering in my heart what I was going to have for lunch. I wanted to go to Tesco first to buy lettuce, but gave up. I said to myself that I could have only a cup of tea and a piece of bread for my lunch. So I went to Mr. and Mrs Bradshaw's house. As I was leaving, Dr. Bradshaw asked me whether I wanted some lettuce. I quickly said 'yes', so he went in the garden and brought me one. I found this very unusual. Of all things, why lettuce? It is easy to give people things such as apples, especially when the donors have lots of apple trees, but why lettuce? The answer is that is what I needed most. But how did he know? This still remains a puzzle to me. Anyway, I went to my house and had my lunch with a piece of bread, lettuce, tomato and cucumber. I was given something to go with my cucumber and tomato. These things are not coincidence; our dear Lord does provide for us.

I had a funny dream on 27.11.93 about 4.30 a.m. I normally dream in the morning. I took this dream to be in the category of seriality. The scene was at my place of work in Hatton Garden, Liverpool. My line manager was checking my work. He said I had put 'not' instead of 'no.' My two workmates were listening, and they laughed. One of them shouted "Oh, she has put 'not'." I did not find it as funny as all that, I just felt sad. I wondered why. Perhaps we are not happy with mistakes.

Next, upon waking, l started working on my book. By then I was writing the chapter on seriality. I started reading my notes again because I had written the chapter some time before, so I was re-reading it in order to connect my points. Interestingly, I came across a sentence which read: "There was a project I wanted to start, but had not money." So I changed 'not' to 'no', then related this to my dream. Most of my dreams don't really need interpretation. The spontaneous element is that what I had written before was part of a conversation between a colleague at work and myself. My colleague asked me on 2.9.93, and I wrote this in the chapter on seriality on the same day when I went to my house. Then I had this dream on 27.11.93.

According to the survey conducted by L.E. Rhine in 1962, as John Beloff puts it, "Examination of a large sample (N=7 119) of spontaneous ESP experiences implicates dreaming as the most frequently reported vehicle of ESP mediation, accounting for approximately 65% of the cases. Furthermore, 85% of the dream experiences, but less than half of the waking experiences, provided complete, as opposed to fragmented or distorted, information."[21]

ESP is not wholly accepted by some psychologists, on the grounds that the knowledge is not based on reason. J.B. Rhine, in his book *New World Of The Mind*, thought it was better to examine their views against psi or ESP. Dr. Lucien Warner, in 1952, conducted a survey when he sent a questionnaire to the Fellows of the American Psychological Association. Of the 360 people who responded, one in six accepted the occurrence of ESP. "89 per cent of those who responded to the questionnaire considered the investigation of ESP a legitimate scientific undertaking and 78 per cent considered it to be within the province of academic psychology."[22] To this end the survey was not ignored but what was rejected were the "results that ESP is a genuine occurrence."[23]

What is clear, as J.B. Rhine puts it, is that "of the five-sixths who rejected the reality of psi, one in three stated that he made up his mind about ESP on a priori grounds, that is, without considering even second-hand reports or reviews of the evidence. In other words, over 30 per cent of these psychologists just knew without any evidence at all, any kind of evidence, that ESP does not occur."[24] Rhine adds that "For them ESP is an impossibility: therefore, there could not be any such thing as an ESP test."[25] Warner and Clark did a similar kind of research in 1938 and came out with a similar percentage.

One of the psychologists, as reported by Rhine, gave his reasons for not accepting ESP. He stated, "I do not accept ESP for a moment, because it does not make sense. My external criteria, both of physics and of physiology, say that ESP is not a fact despite the behavioural evidence that has been reported. I cannot see what other basis my colleagues have for rejecting it; and if they are using my basis, they and I are allowing psychological evidence to be passed on by physical and physiological censors. Rhine may still turn out to be right, improbable as I think that is, and my own rejection of his views in a literal sense prejudice."[26]

The psychologist quoted above spoke on behalf of those who don't accept psi phenomena. Thus Rhine thinks, in his rejection, that "he has told parapsychologists what they have long been needing to know. Now they should understand why they are making such slow headway with the psychology profession. They might wait a long time for a more honest look behind the rejection of the psi evidence than that provided by this quotation."[27] Rhine adds, "It would seem a great pity that nature has overlooked this requirement, and in psi phenomena produced something that is not physical, something that operates in such a manner as to produce psychological evidence. But at least one can see how hard it would be for a thoroughgoing devotee of materialism to accept a factor in man characterised by its non-physical properties."[28]

To my mind, ESP is something to do with believing. If something happens to you, you end up acting on it because the experiential is more important than anything. Jung, however, believed in ESP. Dreams meant a lot to him and he listened to his patients, because he believed the patients did not invent those dreams. It was through a young woman's dream about a scarab that Jung propounded his theory on synchronicity.

Bibliography

1. Koestler, A., *The Roots Of Coincidence*, p. 85, Hutchinson & Co., London, 1972.
2. Koestler, A., *The Ghost in the Machine*, p. 4, Hutchinson London 1967
3. Ibid p. 5
4. Ibid p. 5
5. Inglis, B., *Coincidence: A Matter of Chance – Or Synchronicity?* p. 14, Hutchinson, London, 1990.
6. Koestler, A., et al; *The Challenge Of Chance*, p. 166, Hutchinson, London, 1973.
7. "Ecclesiastes", Chapter 1 v. 9f, RSV.
8. Inglis, B., op. cit p. 16.
9. Hearne, K., *Visions Of The Future*, p. 101, The Aquarian Press, England, 1989.
10. *The Independent*, Wednesday 6.9.94.
11. Jung, C., *The Structure And Dynamics Of The Psyche*, vol. 8 p. 421, Routledge & Kegan Paul, London 1960.
12. Ibid p. 426.
13. Peat, F.D., *"Synchronicity" The Bridge Between Matter & Mind*, p. 26-27, Bantam Books, Toronto, New York, London, Sydney, Auckland 1987.
14. Ibid p. 27.
15. Jung, C., op. cit. p. 426.
16. Jung, C., op. cit. p. 426.
17. Jung, C., op. cit. p. 423-4.
18. Peat, F.D., op. cit. p. 27.
19. Ibid p. 27.
20. Ibid p.27.
21. Beloff, J., *New Direction in Parapsychology* p. 41-42, by Elek Science, London, 1974.

22. Rhine, J.B., *New World Of The Mind*, p. 44, Faber and Faber, 1953.
23. Ibid. p.44.
24. Ibid. p.45.
25. Ibid. p. 45.
26. Ibid. p. 48-49.
27. Ibid. p. 49.
28. Ibid. p. 49-50.

CHAPTER 5

Synchronicity

J ung, as we saw in Chapter 3, seems to adopt his synchronicity
theory from the principle of seriality. Although he dismissed
it, the seriality theory gave him a base on which to propound
his theory. Thus Jung worked in collaboration with Pauli.

Jung was impressed in his research by the writings of the
mediaeval author Mage, who was also a theologian, Albertus
Magnus, who maintained, as Stuart Holroyd asserted in 1977,
that "A certain power to alter things dwells in the human soul
and subordinates the other things to her, particularly when she is
swept into a great excess of love or hate or the like."[1] Holroyd
stated that Jung was interested in the "assertion that a
psychological state can affect events in the physical world without
there being a mechanical cause-effect link between the two
planes, for this was the fundamental assertion of the principle of
synchronicity."[2] The Sufis of India also holds the same belief as
Albertus Magnus.

Creative Activities Corresponding with Each Other

Jung believed synchronistic happenings were the result of the
patterning process in the psyche. He believed in things
corresponding to each other in meaningful relationship. This
was the idea that the macro-cosmos is reflected in the micro-

cosmos. In other words, things of the upper world and earth hold together in hidden affinities. This belief was first stated by Hippocrates. He believed that "there is one common flow, one common breathing, all things are in sympathy."[3]

Koestler, in The *Act of Creation*, also shares this view. He believes that "all creative activities – the conscious and the unconscious processes underlying artistic originality, scientific discovery and a cosmic inspiration have a basic pattern in common."[4] He called this 'bisociative' thinking. Thus he believed that "The interference of two independent series in a given situation is merely a further example of the mechanisation of life."[5]

Jung was also convinced, as Holroyd relates, that "the physical and psychological sciences had been arbitrarily differentiated and must eventually converge, for their fields of investigation, nature and man, matter and mind were justly inter-related and governed by the same fundamental ordering principle."[6]

Later in the book I will describe some events where matter and mind seem to unite. For example, during Jung's death it was as if heaven and earth witnessed his death. Jung had a favourite tree outside his house and the lightning struck it down at the exact time he closed his eyes to rest in peace.

A very interesting example is one that is given by Inglis. Mrs. Hanne O'Rourke, wife of the Irish Ambassador in London, recalls an experience of her uncle at Buchenwald towards the end of the war, when the Germans rounded up members of the Danish police force and took them to concentration camps in Germany. "The toilets were planks over a ditch and the men talked to each other while sitting there. One day my uncle found himself next to a Canadian Air Force officer who had somehow also arrived at the camp. When the Canadian learned that my uncle was Danish, he asked from what part of the country.[7] 'Aarhus' he knew; he might know his wife, Grethe. He produced a photograph of his wife, who had been my uncle's childhood sweetheart."

Events like the above happen most of the time. They have happened to many people. We always say a 'small world'. I went home to Malawi in 1984. I took a bus from Blantyre to my village. It was dark, so I missed my village and came out at a different one. It was so dark that I could not see anything and, with the Mozambique war, it was frightening. I knocked at the door of a house. I did not bother which, so long as they would let me in. However, as I entered, the husband called me by name. I was amazed as to how on earth he knew me. The man had come from our village to marry at that village. We have a matriarchal society. I could not believe this. I was relieved. In the morning his daughter escorted me to my village.

Today, as Inglis puts it, "In the simplest form of coincidence, a 'pair', the chances of its making an impression are strongest if it is so inherently impossible that it suggests some cause other than chance."[8] An eminent American mathematician, Warran Weaver, in his commentary on probability theory, *Lady Luck*, related the story of his next-door neighbour, George D. Bryson. He was travelling in New York and thought of stopping off at Louisville, just to pass some time and to see the city. He enquired about accommodation and went to Brown's Hotel, where he registered. Out of curiosity, he went to the desk to check whether by chance he had any post. The girl at the reception gave him a letter bearing his name, Mr. George D. Bryson, Room 307, and this was the room he was given. The letter was not his, but belonged to the preceding resident.[9] Brian Inglis relates another very interesting story. David Howe, while conducting research in London, 1988, at an agency in a building which accommodated a variety of small-scale arts and business concerns, was chatting with the receptionist while waiting to see the Director. They could hear the sound of a band rehearsing and this made them talk about music. The girl asked him the name of the last record he had bought.

"Ah, I've developed a taste for African music."

"That's one of my interests too."

The last record I bought is by a man from Mali by the name of Ali Farke Toure. I love his music and could hardly believe that his records were available here."

"Look – you're not going to believe this, but he's in the room next door. If you listen carefully you can hear his voice through the wall!"[10]

In 1993, one of the past students of Liverpool University rang me from home asking me if I could go to the Senate House to see a Mr. Gordon about something he wanted. I found this odd, because it would have involved going from office to office asking about him. He did not know the exact office he was in. However, I forced myself to go, especially since the student had taken the trouble to ring from home. So I did not waste time. I stopped at the University and entered the Senate House wondering if I would be able to find him or how to put the message across, since I did not have enough information. However, I went straight to the enquiry desk. While I was mentioning Mr. Gordon's name, the lady at the reception said: "That is Mr. Gordon coming out of that office." So I went straight to him and met him by the door. Thus Vaugham, in his book, *Incredible Coincidence*, 1981, states: "Synchronicity happens to people when they need it. When you don't need it – when your life is secure and stable – it happens rarely. If you live by your wits or in an insecure profession, you will probably find it happening all the time."[11] Vaugham goes on to say, "Things just happen." Or is there, as Jung postulated, an underlying principle of the universe that operates with an importance equal to physical causality?[12] I would add that according to my experience synchronicity happens to us almost every minute but we don't take any notice of it. It's the same as not seeing the blessings God has given us. We don't appreciate because we want more. Sometimes we say we are poor, forgetting that there are some who can't even afford to buy food.

Keep a Thing – It's Use Will Come

It seems also that some of the things which happen to us in very small ways do correspond to our future life. For example, Vaugham gives another interesting story of Lincoln. "One day a stranger came to Lincoln with a barrel full of odds and ends. He said that he was in need of money and that he would be much obliged if Lincoln would help him out by giving him a dollar for the barrel. The contents, he said, were not of much value; they were some old newspapers and things of that sort. But the stranger needed the dollar very badly... Lincoln, with his characteristic kindness, gave the man a dollar for the barrel even though he could not imagine any use that he would have for its contents. Some time later, when he went to clear out the barrel, he found that it contained an almost complete edition of Blackstone's Commentaries. It was the chance, or synchronistic, acquisition of these books that enabled Lincoln to become a lawyer and eventually to embark on his career in politics.[13]

My mother used to tell us not to throw things away but to keep them, saying their use will come. And it used to be so. Some people say everything happens for a reason. Sometimes things seem to go in the wrong direction when in actual fact they are going in the right direction, only we don't know the future. A man named Riche at our church wanted very much to go to theological college, but failed to go for various reasons. He was not happy with the whole situation. In the end it happened that our church minister, Rev. Willie Morris, became very sick for quite a long time. He had an operation. Riche then took over the reverend's work and started preaching. He could now see the reason why he had failed to go to the ministry. The very same thing happens when we want something. Even without saying it, someone gives it to you, as if there is a brain contact. How it happens, only God Almighty knows. My sister back home in Malawi, Victoria, wrote to say she had no blankets. I kept this to myself. Then when I was going for a holiday, Angela Glanville, Principal Development Officer, told me she had some blankets and wondered whether someone at home could make use of them. I was amazed and told her my sister wanted blankets. But I had never told anyone this. Mrs. M. Chikhacizula, a very devoted Christian, always tells me not to tell anyone if I have a problem, but to keep it to myself and pray for it. If you tell people, it is as if you are saying God cannot help. However, things do happen in a strange way.

In both England and America, as Rosalind Heywood asserts, "Experiments conducted under rigid scientific conditions have now shown that it is possible for one human being to become aware at a distance of another's thoughts or feelings, in conditions strictly controlled to ensure that no knowledge of them could have been acquired by sensory means."[14] Evidence has also been produced by some researchers, as Heywood noted. Man is a creature who can make contact with distant events by an unknown process which does not involve the use of sight, hearing, touch, taste or smell, and which to some extent at least is independent of time.[15]

Imagination

A colleague at work, Julie McColl, tells of her synchronistic experience. She writes in her own words, "This is not unusual; it happens about once or twice a week. On 9.5.94., I was thinking about a friend's husband and just wondering how he was and if he had heard his exam results. Within 10 minutes the phone rang and it was he saying he had passed. Again on 10.5.94, 1 followed my conversation with a colleague and later met May Mills. I had been thinking on my way to work about a colleague that used to work with us about two years ago. May stated that she was meeting this colleague for lunch today. I told her I would write this down too."

In this case the moment one is thinking, one is at the same time entering into the process of perceiving. In so doing, one is creating sets of images or bringing memories of the past into one's consciousness. This contemplation, as Lancaster puts it, "retraces the path of this preconscious search. During the moment of contemplation the inhibition of competing representations is suspended as we become conscious of material brought forward by this search through the memory store."[16] Julie McColl was considering how her friend was doing and especially how the exams went. What she was doing was retrieving memories of what she knew already. Even so, the question of how one can think of someone who rings you during the very time of contemplating still remains a mystery. Lancaster attributes this to something 'absolute' and contends that this 'absolute' results "in all things merging together in a kind of primordial idea."[17] Blake also declared, as quoted by Lancaster, "If the doors of perception were cleansed, everything would appear to man as it is, infinite."[18] Blake also asserted, "The object's reality lies in its totality, which emerges only with its deeper fusion with everything else."[19]

Arising from the above, Lancaster believes that "all things are connected in the implicate order. Since our consciousness also is founded in the implicate order, contemplation would imply retracting our connection to things."[20] This also relates to the idea that things are connected like a chain. Some believe there must surely be an external force. Lancaster then concludes: "Whether or not we embrace such overtly religious terms, we find more and more evidence for the notion that the basic principle of the psyche is the creative imagination."[21]

Loud Detonation

An unknown reader, Miss Margaret Green of London W1, wrote to Koestler, as Koestler himself states in the *Challenge of Chance*: "Reading your ... book, *The Roots of Coincidence*, yesterday morning on the way to Cambridge by train, I came upon the story of the loud detonation in Freud's bookcase during his talk with Jung. Long ago I had known that there was a fundamental clash of temperamental forces between these two thinkers, and I was intrigued by the story.[22]

"On the way back in the train in the evening I had your book with me and the story of the detonations kept on coming back, with amusement, into my mind. About twenty minutes before getting to Liverpool Street, there was a sudden bang, like a bomb, and splinters of glass flew round the carriage and there was a jagged hole in the big window. My attention and that of the other two unknown people in the carriage, was taken up with shaking glass off ourselves and each other, and it was not, I think, until this morning that, again with amusement, the coincidence occurred to me."[23]

Frightened by a Leopard

I was driving along Salima Road (in Malawi) with a friend of mine, in 1974 or 1975. It was a long journey from Salima to Blantyre. There were massive trees on the road at that time. We stopped to pass water. I was frightened by the atmosphere. The bush was so terrible that we did not dare to go far from the car, so we just stood by the car passing water. My friend said, "We have to be quick because we don't know what sort of an animal can jump on us." Before she finished the sentence, there was an animal, which we thought was a leopard, coming from the very top of a tree and, thank God, it made a tremendous noise as if to alert us. We jumped into the car and my friend drove off quickly. For a moment we were both silent; we could not talk. After travelling some distance further, she said, "That's what I was telling you. You don't stand by these big trees. My friend was from Salima so she knew what she was talking about. But even if she had not told me to be quick, I would not have stood there for long. There was in me a feeling of sensation or imagination. Actually it was odd for us to stop there.

A Snake in my Legs

My mother and I experienced another incident. My maternal aunt, who is now dead, was married in Mozambique. We used to walk a long distance to reach my maternal aunt's place, probably taking the whole day to do so. I was then quite small, probably twelve years old. Being little myself, I had to be in front in case something attacked me at the back. While we were walking on this small path, my mother noticed I was walking with my eyes looking ahead not looking at the ground. So she said, "Mary, try to look at the ground when walking; don't just look ahead. A snake can bite you." Before she finished the sentence, there was a snake coming from the bush entering that small path. My mother saw it quickly; it was coming towards my legs. She pulled me hastily back saying, "This snake would have bitten you." Such then is an example of synchronicity.

Synchronicity Defined Through a Song

I was also fascinated by a song called 'Synchronicity' with words and music by Sting, Magnetic Publishing Ltd. 1983. It flows nicely like a poem and expresses the real meaning of synchronicity. The words are as follows:

> "With one breath, with one flow,
> You will know
> Synchronicity.
>
> A connecting Principle
> Linked to the invisible,
> Almost imperceptible.
> Something Inexpressible,
> Logic so inflexible,
> Causally connectable,
> Yet nothing is invincible.
>
> If we share this nightmare,
> Then we can dream
> Spiritus mundi.
>
> If you act as you think,
> The missing link,
> Synchronicity.
>
> We know you, they know me,
> Extrasensory
> Synchronicity.

A star fall, a phone call,
It joins all,
Synchronicity.

It's so deep, it's so wide,
You're inside
Synchronicity.

Effect without a cause,
sub-atomic laws, scientific pause,
Synchronicity...

Talk of the Devil

Thinking about the subject one night, I came to remember about the resurrection of Jesus Christ. Interestingly enough, it was during Lenten time, the 'Passion' week. I asked myself why there is so much argument when the Bible tells it to us so simply. On the day of the resurrection the two disciples, whilst on their way to Emmaus, were worried and talking about our Lord Jesus Christ. Whilst they were talking, Jesus appeared to them. He drew near and asked them, "What is this conversation which you are holding with each other as you walk?" They stood still, looking sad. Then one of them, named Cleopas, answered him, "Are you the only visitor to Jerusalem who does not know the things that have happened there in these days?' Lk 24 v.18 (RSV). Jesus asked 'what things?' And they said to him, "Concerning Jesus of Nazareth, who was a prophet mighty in deed and word before God and all the people, and how our chief priests and rulers delivered him up to be condemned to death, and crucified him." Jesus started relating the whole history to them, beginning with Moses and all the prophets. He interpreted to them all the scriptures, the things concerning himself, but still they did not recognise him.

When they reached the village they insisted that Jesus should stay with them since it was dark. He went with them. When he sat at the table with them, "He took the bread and blessed it and broke it and gave it to them. And their eyes were opened and they recognised him, and he vanished out of their sight. Lk 24 v.30 (RSV). They rose and rushed to Jerusalem and found that the eleven disciples had already gathered together. They related the story to them including the breaking of the bread.

The appearance of the Lord to them was purely psychic. The disciples were very worried. They talked about nothing but Jesus who was crucified. They were sad and were worried as to whether Jesus had indeed risen. No doubt they thought it was probably the end of everything. All of a sudden Jesus appeared to them. Jesus appeared to them because the two disciples had first talked about him. This was not just a coincidence. If it were, then it was a meaningful coincidence. He would not have appeared to them if they had not mentioned his name.

Jesus appeared to them for a reason – to take away their worry and doubt and to strengthen them, actually to say he had risen. So what I am saying is this: you have to talk or think of the person and then in a minute that person appears. Sometimes you talk of something which you have not even thought of – a slip of the tongue perhaps; in the final analysis, you find, that too, has a meaning. Freud believed that even that slip of the tongue refers to some hidden thoughts. It is in these circumstances that I believe there are some guiding angels. It is a pity that some of the writings of the apostles were left out. Otherwise we might have heard stories about angels surrounding Jesus during the time of the crucifixion and after the resurrection. God himself also plays a great role in psychic phenomena. With the example given, I am more and more inclined to think that some supernatural powers or divination play a part in psychic matters. We do not recognise those things we do not want to know. The subject of the psyche has already been discussed in the first chapter.

Empirical Nature

Carl Jung, in his book, *Synchronicity*, pointed out that "Both Geulincx and Leibnitz regarded the coordination of the psychic and the physical as an act of God, of some principle standing outside empirical nature."[24] Some psychologists do call these coincidences a combination of 'nature' and 'psychic' This is related to the idea of divination.

Alister Hardy et al., in the *Challenge of Chance*, as John Beloff asserts in his book review, also holds this view concerning nature. "Somewhere in the interstices between causality on the one hand (be it normal or paranormal), and pure chance on the other, there lies a fundamental principle or nature still waiting to be recognised which can best, I think, be described as a principle of meaningful coincidences, a principle whereby events can meaningfully be related even though they are causally unconnected or have no common causal origin."[25]

Van der Post had a vision or psychic experience at the time Carl Jung died. Brian Inglis related the story: "Between sleeping and waking one afternoon on a liner returning to Britain from South Africa, Laurens Van der Post had a vision of himself in avalanche country, filled with the fore-knowledge of imminent disaster."[26] Brian Inglis quotes the exact words of Van der Post. "Suddenly, at the far end of the valley on a Matterhorn peak of my vision, still caught in the light of the sun, Jung appeared. He stood there briefly, as I had seen him some weeks before at the gate, at the end of the garden of his house, then waved his hand at me and called out, 'I'll be seeing you.' Then he vanished down the far side of the mountain."[27] Van der Post continues relating his experience. The next morning, when Van der Post looked through his cabin porthole, as Inglis puts it, he still witnessed Jung's death. "I saw a great white lone albatross gliding by, the sun on fire on its wings. As it glided by, it turned its head and looked straight at me. I had done that voyage countless times before and such a thing had never happened to me, and I had a feeling as if some tremendous ritual had been performed. Hardly had I got back into bed, when my steward appeared with a tray of tea and fruit and, as he always did, the ship's radio news. I opened it carefully. The first item I saw was the announcement that Jung had died the previous afternoon at his home in Zurich. Taking into consideration the time, the latitude and longitude of the ship's position, it was clear that my dream, or vision, had come to me at the moment of his death."[28]

The events described above happened at exactly the same time that Carl Jung was dying. Van der Post was far away in the ship, nowhere near Zurich. But still he experienced, or saw in a vision, Carl Jung's death. No one can deny that this was the act of God or a guardian angel, telling him that his friend was in agony struggling with death. That could never be just a coincidence or chance.

Meeting Each Other in Amsterdam

I must give another example of synchronicity which I found very strange. I was preparing to visit Malawi for the Christmas of 1992 and had already bought my ticket. There was a girl whom I once taught at Secondary School in Malawi. She was a very lovely and polite girl and she was also very beautiful. It was not so much her beauty that attracted me as her politeness. The girl became part of us, to the extent that although a friend, she was like a niece. Thus she was bridesmaid at the wedding of my cousin.

I had not seen this girl for almost sixteen years. I had not written to her but had made up my mind that I had to make an effort to go and see her during my visit to Malawi. I could not get her out of my mind. I was contemplating how I could see her. She lived in Lilongwe, the Capital of Malawi, and I lived in a village quite far from the town. I had gone to see my mother who was sick, so she was my first priority and there was no need for me to hang around in the town. I left the matter as it was and believed a solution would be found when I reached home.

I set off for Malawi on the 13th January, 1993. I took a KLM flight from Manchester to Amsterdam. On arrival in Amsterdam,

I went straight to the gate where the plane for Malawi was to arrive. As I approached the airport lounge, there was a girl sitting facing the direction I was coming from. Although there were other people there, I could only see the girl from Lilongwe in my mind. I went straight over to greet her, without even putting my luggage down. I suppose this was due to my excitement at seeing her. At first she hesitated as she did not recognise me. Apparently, she only knew it was me when I spoke because she remembered the gap between two of my teeth. I wondered why I thought of her in particular and how we could come to meet like this. It was as though she was waiting there for me.

I found this incident unique. It could be explained or described as something inexpressible, to steal William James' word. Jung, in his book, *Synchronicity*, described these psychic phenomena as "absolutely unique and ephemeral events whose existence we have no means of either denying or proving and which can never be the object of empirical science."[29] I do not know whether the incident could be described as a coincidence or just chance. Jung stated, "Chance, we say, must obviously be susceptible of some causal explanation and is only called 'chance' or 'coincidence' because its causality has not yet been discovered."[30] Jung goes on to say that "Since we have an inveterate conviction of the absolute validity of causal law, we regard this explanation of chance as being adequate."[31] Perhaps meaningful coincidences or chance, i.e. a-causal connection, are very natural.

Flammarion, the astronomer, and others related the problem of chance to telepathy. Flammarion was also the first to link other suspicious happenings with the general interest in phenomena connected with death. Thus, he relates, as Jung puts it, "that, while writing his book on the atmosphere, he was just at the chapter on wind force when a sudden gust of wind swept all his papers off the table and blew them out of the window."[32]

These coincidences are hard to understand. I would say that more explanation of extra-sensory-perception (ESP) is needed in order to take full account of them. Jung says that "effect cannot be understood as anything except a phenomenon of energy.

Therefore it cannot be a question of cause and effect, but of a falling together in time, a kind of simultaneity."[33] Because of this quality of simultaneity, Jung used the term 'synchronicity' to designate a hypothetical factor equal in rank to causality as a principle of explanation. In his essay, 'The Spirit of Psychology', Jung defined synchronicity as "a psychically conditioned relativity of time and space."[34] Rhine's experiments, on the other hand, "show that in relation to psyche, space and time are, so to speak, 'elastic' and can apparently be reduced almost to vanishing point, as though they were dependent on psychic conditions and did not exist in themselves but were only 'postulated' by the conscious mind."[35]

In December, 1992, my nephew and I went to a travel agent to buy a ticket to travel to my home town in Malawi, as I had received word that my mother was sick. At first I was told that there were no cheap flights until 31st January. This made it very difficult for me to tell my family when I planned to arrive. I was told by the agent that they would keep checking to see if there were any cheaper flights available. I eventually managed to book my flight with KLM. I was so excited about returning home, but had the problem of telling my family when I would arrive. If I sent a letter it would not reach them in time, especially as it was a Bank Holiday. I explained to my nephew that I needed one of my family to telephone me so that I could tell them the arrangements. We returned to my house and after half an hour the telephone rang. It was indeed my brother-in-law ringing me. In the sixteen years that I had lived in Britain this was the first time he had telephoned me. Why should he ring me on this particular day and hour, especially at the time that I was so desperate and more importantly only thirty minutes after I had said I wished someone from home would ring me? Examples such as this have led me to believe in the guardian angels.

Although I do not believe this occurrence to be merely coincidence, I connected the aforementioned examples with the definition given by Carl Jung himself: "synchronicity, therefore, means the simultaneous occurrence of certain psychic states with one or more external events which appear as meaningful parallels to the momentary subjective state and in certain cases vice-versa."[36]

The occurrence originated within the realm of my psyche wishing that someone from my family would ring me. The internal, or rather the unconscious, mind was connected to the conscious mind, producing the external event, that of the telephone call. In this case we could deduce that the unconscious knows more than the conscious.

It would not be wrong if I mention that I am, to some extent, prone to coincidences and that they usually appear in a more mundane way. Each day brings a coincidence of its own. No matter how small it is, it is still meaningful to me. On Sunday, 20th July, 1993, I had been to church, and went back home for a light lunch. I was worried about one of my colleagues; I had not seen her for two weeks. I wondered whether she had gone away since the university students were on holiday.

I was going to read in Sefton Park and I told my nephew, "If a friend rings, tell her I will be back by 5.00 p. m., so she can come to have tea with us." It was already 2.00 p.m. as I was going. An idea came to me that perhaps it would be better to go to her first before going to the park to read. I went and rang the bell. The nuns with whom she was staying told me she was on the phone ringing her friend. I knew she was ringing my house and that she was talking to my nephew, so I waited. When she finished talking on the phone, she saw me and was excited and said, "Oh Mary: I was just ringing your house."

I found this amazing. What a coincidence? Looking at the timing, it seems to me that at the time I was talking to my nephew about her, she was already going down the stairs to ring me. She lives very near to me. I must admit I really found this incident very interesting and remembered what Brian Inglis said about spontaneous happenings. In his book, *The Unknown Quest*, he asserts that "Nobody would be likely to dispute that they can provide us with timely warnings of a kind which we cannot consciously account for."[37] Given this statement, Inglis wonders whether these should be called Extra-Sensory-Communications (ESC), instead of Extra Sensory Perception. Inglis is of the opinion that the "conscious self is capable of picking up transmissions of the kind which, when they reach consciousness, we call premonitions."[38]

It was also on Sunday, 29th August, 1993, that I went to visit Mrs. Rosemary Mujewa, from Uganda. She works for the Liverpool City Council as an occupational therapist. While there I enquired how Rev. John Kyazze was doing. He is a Catholic priest, and at the moment taking a doctorate degree at Manchester University. I had met him once at Rosemary's house. Rosemary responded by saying she had not seen him for quite a long time. Within five minutes the bell rang and I had the feeling it must be Rev. Kyazze. Why I thought it was he I don't know. Rosemary went to open the door and said, "Mary was just asking about you." The priest, as if he knew what was in my mind, said, "Now I have given you something to write in your book."

The above examples have left a great impression on me. Thus coincidences, I would say, do happen for a reason. As I have shown, they are not subjective since other people are also involved. Jung made it clear, in fact, that "It is a transcendental, not a subjective concept of meaning" that he is talking about. Indeed at one point, as Beloff observed, Jung suggests that "synchronicity may be regarded as standing alongside space, time, causality and energy as a fundamental dimension of objective reality."[39]

I believe that an explanation for these coincidences could be that some kind of natural law is guiding us. I have yet another incident which I believe was a miracle, and in which a guardian angel was involved. Early in 1977 I went to Kitwe, in Zambia, to do a course in women's leadership. When the course ended, I decided to go to Lusaka before flying to Malawi. I booked a place at the Young Women's Christian Association (YWCA), intending to stay for only one night, and then go to stay with my cousin, Betty Ndau. However, I did not have her home address, only the hospital address where she was working. She was working at the

Lusaka Teaching Hospital. The hospital was very near to the YWCA, so after I had got my keys to the hostel, I went to look for my cousin. I didn't even know whether she would be able to recognise me as she had last seen me as a little girl. I went to look for her, but no one seemed to know her so I returned to the hostel.

The following day was a Sunday. I was frustrated that I had not managed to see her, so I slept on the problem and in the morning decided to attend the first church I could find, regardless of its denomination. On my way to find a church, I went window shopping. This is because I could not find any church, so I gave up the idea of going to a service. Since there was nothing I could do, I stood somewhere outside a shop, and I was concentrating so much on the things in the shop window that I did not notice the group of women passing behind me on their way to the Salvation Army Church. After they had gone past some distance, one of the women shouted, "Is that you Mary?" I turned around to find that it was another one of my cousins. If it had been the one I went to look for at the hospital, some would argue that perhaps she heard from her colleagues at the hospital that someone was looking for her. Another point is that these two cousins lived in different villages. So in no way would she have perceived that I was there in Lusaka. Sometimes you can recognise a person if you know she is around. But it was not so in this case.

I knew that this particular cousin had left Malawi, but I had no idea which country she had gone to. She said, "Even though I only saw your back, I knew that it must be Mary. A relative is a relative; you cannot miss her." I was puzzled and at the same time filled with sadness without knowing why. It was as if I was saying, "Who am I for the Lord to take care of me?" To me it was not just a coincidence but some supernatural power or a guiding angel.

She invited me to accompany them to their church. I asked her, "What denomination is that?" and she said, 'Salvation Army'. I had never heard of this church before, so I hesitated, but she insisted that I go with them. She said I was going to enjoy the service and the singing in particular. She introduced me to her friends, and I did indeed enjoy the service, especially the singing. It was the first time I had listened to the Salvation Army service, because at that time we did not have it in Malawi.

When the service had ended, she took me to Betty, my older cousin, whom I had been looking for in the first place. My cousin was very surprised to see me, because she had only seen me when I was very young. She was also surprised to see me there in Zambia. However, her family put together a big welcome meal. They killed a big chicken and went out to buy ox liver. In Malawi one feels welcome only if they kill a chicken. They all wanted me to stay the night but I had to decline as I was flying to Malawi the following day. They escorted me back to the YWCA, where I had arranged to stay the night. The following morning I took a taxi to the airport and went to my country, Malawi. In my view the above account was not just chance, coincidence or synchronicity, but an event in which I was guided by an angel to meet my cousin. My cousin was puzzled too. She could hardly believe the fact that I was in that particular street. Her friends were also stunned by the whole occurrence. Moreover, one of the women revealed, "We do not normally take this road; we go by the other side. Today the Lord wanted us to take this road in order to meet you."

Jung gave a very good example of synchronicity by explaining a dream of one of his young female patients. In the dream the woman was given a golden scarab. The woman was describing the dream to Jung as he was sitting by a window, when all of a sudden he turned around to see an insect knocking against the window pane from the outside. Jung opened the window and caught the insect as it flew in. The woman then explained to him that it was the same shape as the golden scarab in her dream. Jung was amazed by this and failed to understand how such a thing could happen. The insect was of a species analogous to the golden scarab.

Predicting the Death of a Secret Agent

Another good example of this type of psychic phenomenon is that given by Peter Hurkos in his book *Psychic*. Hurkos was in a Netherlands hospital after he had been knocked down and made unconscious in an accident. While he was recovering in hospital, a British secret agent, who had finished his treatment and was about to be discharged, came over to Hurkos to say farewell. The agent shook hands with Hurkos and that instant Hurkos learned something about him just by touch. He believed that the British agent was soon to be killed by the Germans on Kalver Street. Hurkos cried out to the agent warning him not to leave the hospital. The agent left and Hurkos continued shouting his fate but nobody listened. They thought that he must be mentally disturbed to make such claims. A nurse who was in the room rushed to Hurkos' bedside and asked him what was the matter. Hurkos found himself staring intently at the stranger as though he was in shock.

The stranger nervously muttered to the nurse: "for such a sick man, he has the strength of a bull." With these words the British agent left the room. Hurkos shouted, "Stop him, he is going to be killed. He's a British agent and the Germans know about him. He will be killed on Kalver Street. Stop him, stop him!"[40] A doctor who had also heard the disturbance rushed in and, with a nurse, gently forced Hurkos back into a reclining position in bed. After Hurkos had regained consciousness the nurse and the doctor warned him that he must take things easy, explaining that he had a serious skull fracture. They told him to rest and not to become too excited.

Two days later, after his release from the hospital, the British agent, who had been parachuted into Holland, was killed by the Gestapo in Kalver Street, as Hurkos had predicted and futilely warned. Following the death of the agent, the underground movement quickly learned from the doctors and nurses that Hurkos had predicted his death. After the incident the doctors and nurses put Hurkos in contact with the hospital psychiatrist, Dr. Perters, who examined him every day.

An Image of a Dead Person Covering the Window

A very respectable lady at our church, who is in her seventies, told me yet another strange story. Her uncle, Jack Winstanley, had a son who used to spend his holiday with this lady's family. Later on the son moved to London and when the Second World War broke out he went to Germany to fight. Jack had already died by this time. One day the lady experienced something that she can remember vividly to this day. She went into her sitting room to find an image of her uncle Jack covering the entire window pane. She was terrified and fled upstairs to her bedroom, wondering what such an occurrence could possibly mean.

A week passed and she received a telegram informing her that Jack's son had died in Germany. The lady believes that the time she saw the vision of her uncle was the exact time that her uncle's son died in Germany. Keith Hearne, in his book, *Visions of the Future*, states that "There are often great difficulties in deciding whether a psi experience was distinctly precognitive or simultaneous. The timing is of crucial relevance in classification. If something unexpected happens, it is a matter of determining precisely when it occurred and how sudden it was in relation to the received information."[41] In this case, the time that she saw her uncle's picture on the window was the same time that his son died. The information took a week to reach her because the process of identifying the person and his address is a lengthy one.

Omen

An event concerning an omen is told by Jung himself. The wife of one of his patients told him a story. He explained, "At the death of her mother and her grandmother, a number of birds gathered outside the windows of the death-chamber."[42] Jung sent the husband to a specialist to check on his symptoms, which pointed to a heart disease. The specialist concluded that there was no cause for anxiety, thus returning the patient to Jung. While the man was returning from the specialist, he collapsed. As he was brought into the hospital, his wife was already in a state of panic because soon after her husband had gone to the doctor, a large flock of birds had landed on their house, as they had done twice before. These are not just coincidences, but I believe them to be the effect of some kind of angelic guidance. On seeing the birds, the wife of the patient was filled with fear, because the same thing had happened when her mother and grandmother died. All three of these occurrences have a meaning. These coincidences are seen by some as unintelligible objects. They have indicated or signalled to a number of us that they are rational or intellectual phenomena. They are very helpful indeed, since they illustrate a happening before it actually occurs.

Threefold Unity

It is believed by some that things are connected in a chain. Jung refers this statement to a quotation by Pico Della Mirandola, when he talks of a simple threefold unity, and compares it to the doctrine of the Trinity. According to Pico's view, this threefold unity does not depart from 'unity distinguished by a threefold character'. However, simple threefold unity is described as follows: "Firstly, there is the unity in things whereby each thing is at one with itself, consists of itself, and coheres with itself. Secondly, there is the unity whereby one creature is united with the others of the world and constitutes one world. The third and most important unity is that whereby the whole universe is one with its Creator, as an army with its commander."[43] This, I think, relates to the fact that the universe is round, meaning if you start from this end and travel continuously you will end the journey by reaching the same place. Koestler, in *The Act of Creation*, holds the same principle. He believes all creation activities have a basic pattern in common, as mentioned earlier on.

From the simple threefold unity which Pico describes, he saw the world as "One being, a visible God, in which everything is naturally arranged from the very beginning like the parts of a living organism. The world appears as the Corpus Mysticum of God, just as the Church is the Corpus Mysticum of Christ, or as a well-disciplined army can be called a sword in the hand of the commander. The view that all things are arranged according to God's will is one that leaves little room for causality. Just as in a living body the different parts work in harmony, are meaningfully adjusted to another, so events in the world stand in a meaningful relationship which cannot be derived from any imminent causality. [44] That things are naturally arranged seems to create some problems since this seems to refer to the doctrine of predestination. However, Pico himself was well aware of this problem, and says at the end of his quote, that to say that things are naturally arranged leaves little room for causality."[45]

All Things in Harmony

However, Hippocrates, the Greek philosopher, as Jung asserted, believed, "There is one common flow, one common breathing, all things are in sympathy. The whole organism and each one of its parts are working in conjunction for the same purpose... the great principle extends to the most extreme part, and from the extremest part it returns to the great principle, to the one nature, being and not being."[46] Most of the things which happen in this field refer to nature. It is as if the devil has blinded us so that we are unable to use or recognise God's manifestation.

Agrippa, an older contemporary of Theophrastus Paracelsus, shares the same view as the Platonists. This view is that "There is an imminent power in the things of the upper world."[47] This power I have designated as God acting in a miraculous way through the guardian angels. Agrippa quoted Virgil, as Jung stated, "I for my part do not believe that they are endowed with divine spirit or with a foreknowledge of things greater than the oracle."[48]

An Inborn Knowledge

Agrippa thus suggested, "There is an inborn 'knowledge' or 'imagination' in living organisms, an idea which recurs in our own day from Hans Driesch."[49] Freud also talked of the inborn knowledge, as Arkinson et al., put it, "Because each of us is born with these impulses, they exert a pervasive influence that must be dealt with in some manner."[50] Agrippa added, "It is certainly not our knowledge as we know it, but rather as self-subsistent," unconscious knowledge which I would prefer to call 'absolute knowledge'[51], absolute' meaning that true knowledge has not been exaggerated.

Leibnitz chose to call it 'perceiving' or consisting of images of subjectless 'simulacra' Jung suggested these images could be compared to the idea of 'archetypes', "which can be shown to be formal factors in spontaneous fantasy products."[52] Also that these are expressed in modern language, "The microcosm which contains the images of all creation would be collectively unconscious."[53] The idea of inborn knowledge seems to be accepted by some writers. The more I tend to agree with this view, the more I think the view is similar to reincarnation. For someone to have inborn knowledge might seem to indicate that he/she existed before; perhaps this is possible in terms of genetics only. Jung, however, as I have shown in *The Usefulness of Dreams*, believed he lived before to the extent of remembering that he was a historian and God recreated him to be a psychologist or to finish unfinished business. However, our knowledge is limited so that we cannot really know these paranormals unless our dear Lord reveals them to us. Perceiving also seems to create some difficulties. One of the philosophers, Jean-Paul Sartre, seems to have suggested that what we perceive is what we already know. This also applies to the card game, as already explained in the previous chapter. Having said this, many people do actually perceive things. I perceived my own mother's death, as has already been discussed in Chapter 1. This is why I have always maintained it is God. The idea of the inborn knowledge seems to equate with Jung's idea of the archetype. Some, on the other hand, would prefer to call perceiving 'imagining'. This also depends on their experiences.

Jung suggested that Agrippa was describing the unconscious mind. Jung then states that the spirit that "penetrates all things, or shapes all things, is the world soul." The soul of the world is, therefore, the only certain thing, filling all things, bestowing all things, binding and knitting together all things, that it might make one frame of the world. Those things in which the spirit is particularly powerful, therefore, have a tendency to 'beget their like', in other words to produce correspondences of meaningful coincidences.[54]

Psychic Powers

Agrippa talks of the 'imminent power', as already mentioned. However, imminent power might mean different things to different people. Some would associate it with any power or a 'bang', whilst some would associate it with the supernatural power, in this sense 'God'. As has always been my theme, this supernatural power I have termed 'angelic guidance'. In this sense it is God operating in these angels. When something happens and you just mention it before it actually happened, your friends ask you, "How did you know?" I just mentioned it and I don't know how I came to mention it. A certain lady told me of a similar experience. She writes in her own words, "During the summer, one very hot night, I couldn't sleep very well so I was listening to the radio, and I thought the radio news reader said that Bob Marley collapsed and died from cancer of the brain. I told everyone at work about it the next day as it was a shock to me; I was a fan of Bob Marley's. No one else had heard about it and after several days of no further news about it, I believed I was going mad. A couple of weeks later Bob Marley did collapse and die with a brain tumour."

A good example is given of Lawrence's experience by Puharich. "Dr. Lawrence entered his office promptly at eight-thirty. He nodded good morning to his dental assistant and quickly walked to his desk. He sat down and began thumbing through his morning mail. Suddenly a thought struck him. He had an idea which he wanted to share immediately with his research associate, Bill Harmon. He reached over to the telephone and began dialling Bill's number. Bill Harmon, at this very instant, was still asleep in bed. He awoke abruptly with one thought on his mind, 'call Joe Lawrence.' Acting immediately in his ear, Joe was already saying, 'Hello'. The telephone bell had not rung."[55]

I was talking to one of the Divisional Service Managers at work, Maria Wrigley. I was telling her about the story of someone who went to the dentist. The man who went to the dentist related his story to one of the writers in parapsychology and this writer put it in his book. The story is very interesting and we were all laughing. While we were laughing about this dentist story, a telephone rang. It was one of the residential officers telling her that she was going to the dentist.

Transference Thoughts

In 1935, three years before he died, Freud was asked by a Hungarian writer, Cornelius Tabori, about his understanding of the question of paranormal phenomena. Freud replied, "The transference of thoughts, the possibility of sensing the past or the future cannot merely be accidental."[56]

In their book, *Dreams the Language of the Unconscious*, Cayce et al. define perception' as "the translation of an impulse transmitted through one or a combination of the senses into an awareness of the thing being perceived."[57] But I still think that you do not have to perceive things; rather you comprehend them by your intuition. This comprehension starts from inside you. As such, it is the work of angelic guidance. If we want to talk about things being perceived, then one would argue that what we perceive is what we already know.

Another interesting story is about a church choir. This account was given by Lyall Watson in a book called *Earthworks*. The choir used to gather at half-past-seven on fixed dates. It was in March, 1950 That everyone in the choir was late. The minister's wife, whose role was to play the piano, was busy ironing her daughter's dress. The soprano was doing her geometry homework. Another member could not staff the car. The two tenors were watching the end of a sports programme. The bass singer overslept after taking a nap. The church they were to sing at was wrecked by a devastating explosion at seven twenty-five.[58]

To explain the above account as a mere coincidence or chance is implausible to my mind. Some supernatural or angelic powers played a role in this case. Surely, if this occurrence was due to chance, one of the members would have turned up.

A Small World

Timothy Walker gave me two coincidences which he found very fascinating. "Whilst living in Clapton, East London, I was asked to go and teach English in Stockholm for two weeks. I had never been north of Scotland and, coming from Malawi, the idea of going as far north as Sweden was certainly something. On the evening before leaving, I packed my bags and realised that if I did not go out for a drink at the local pub, I would not be able to get to sleep, as my mind was racing. The nearest local, as it happened, was not all that congenial a place, so when I stepped out of the front door I decided to go in the opposite direction to reach the nearest pub easily. I soon found a different pub tucked away on a side street and the quiet atmosphere seemed appropriate. While having a pint and reading a book, I noticed a young African man enter the pub and order a lager. He somehow did not have the bearing of a Londoner and this intrigued me. As luck would have it, we got into conversation and he told me that he came from a small country in Africa that no one had ever heard of. I asked him to be more specific and when he said Malawi, I said 'Muli bwanji' and gave him a bit of a shock. He was waiting in the pub for his brother who turned up about half an hour later. I greeted him in the same manner with the same result. What is intriguing about this chance encounter is that Malawi and Africa were much on my mind. Sweden had always taken a close interest in African affairs and now I had the opportunity of visiting that country. For some reason I decided not to go to the nearest pub, which I would usually have done if simply looking for a quick beer. I ventured off elsewhere and literally allowed other doors to be opened. Meeting these two Malawian brothers in London made me aware of the lives they and others were leading."

The second story which Timothy Walker gives began in England and concluded in Malawi. "One day, whilst a student at Sussex University, I hitchhiked from London back to Brighton. Just south of London a woman gave me a lift as far as the Thornton Heath area. I mentioned that I came from Malawi and she told me that she had been there for a holiday. As the conversation continued, it turned out that she had gone to Malawi to visit her sister and brother-in-law and that one evening they had met my parents, who live in Malawi. This meeting in Malawi was a chance meeting as my parents did not know the other couple very well at that time. The coincidence seemed incredible and we put it down to the fact that 'It's a small world'."

A 'Pun' Coincidence

Allan Combs et al. give an example of synchronistic occurrence which involved a pun and which took place in Texas. It was about a state highway patrolman who was badly injured by a motorcycle. Allan Falby struck the back of a truck and was thrown to the road. Alfred Smith stopped from his car to assist. Smith discovered Falby was bleeding heavily from one leg. He used his tie as a tourniquet, and Smith managed to stop the bleeding and in a way saved Falby's life. Since then the two men never met until two years later when Smith had a car accident this time and was severely injured. As a coincidence, Falby was the first to arrive on the scene. Like Smith, Falby applied a tourniquet to stop bleeding. Only after the bleeding had stopped did Falby recognise it was Smith, the business man who had also saved Falby's life.

Falby then, as Allan Combs et al. put it, passed a joke: "One good tourniquet deserves another."[59]

The above is Honegger's interpretation of synchronicity. As in regard to the Freudian tradition, Honegger emphasises hidden linguistic relationships, in this case a pun. In another example she relates synchronistic to 'hidden verbal meanings.'

Another coincidence is given by Grattan-Guinness. He related a number of coincidences which happened to Charles Osborne, of the Caulfield Institute of Technology, Melbourne, who was researching with colleagues on the metallurgy of (apparently) psychically bent metal. Here is the coincidence: "Toronto, August, 1961. I spent some months there before returning to England via New York. 'Goodbye Edgar', I said to a friend who was leaving to take up theological studies in New York City somewhere, 'I'll see you in New York City then'. My remark surprised me as much as him, but there he was on the pavement six weeks later when I was looking around Columbia University."[60]

The above account is very interesting. I think Charles Osborne said it out of the blue or it was a slip of the tongue, as Freud might suppose. Guinness calls it 'conscious anticipation-made'. I am still inclined to call this event an act of a guardian angel. 'Even if it is something anticipated, New York is a big city and would seem to make chances of them meeting remote. There is truly an observer in heaven, who sees all that we plan to do.

Needless to say, the theory of synchronicity has not gained much credibility with outsiders. A Jung psychiatrist, M.L. Franz, gave a very convincing example. "A woman with a very strong power complex and a 'devouring' attitude towards people, dreamt of seeing three tigers seated threateningly in front of her. Her analyst pointed out the meaning of the dream and, through causal arguments, tried to make her understand the devouring attitude she thus displayed. Later in the day the patient and her friend, while strolling along Lake Zurich, noticed a crowd gazing at three tigers in a barn – most unusual inhabitants of a Swiss barn."[61]

Montague Ullman et al. commented, "The three tigers were in

the barn because a circus was spending the night in town."[62] However, as Franz points out, "the highly improbable coincidence of the inner and outer tigers in this woman's life... inevitably struck her as 'more than mere chance' and somehow meaningful."[63]

Intelligible Things Without a Brain

Most of us have connected psychic phenomena with the brain. The whole idea is that you think or talk of something and it suddenly happens. Lancaster also believes that the association of the imagery and perception "may be placed on a firmer foundation by reference to evidence that imagery shares brain mechanisms with perception."[64] Jung, however, felt "We must completely give up the idea of the psyche's being somehow connected with the brain, and remember instead the 'meaningful' or 'intelligent' behaviour of the lower organisms, which are without a brain."[65]

I was intrigued by another coincidence, which I thought involved brain relationship. One of the Social Workers at Liverpool Drug Dependency Clinic shared with me a very interesting story. She told me that each time she wants to buy a present for her brother, she finds that her sister has also bought a present for him, usually the very same one she had bought. On one occasion they both bought a book for him of the same title. Also when she buys a dress and visits home, she finds her sister wearing the same dress. I was impressed and asked her whether they were twins. She replied "No, there are five years between us."

Another colleague, one of the training officers, Ros Burton, bought a present for her mother (a jumper), but was disappointed when she went to deliver the present to find that her mother had also bought her the same present.

Criticism of Synchronicity

Although there is a wealth of evidence given by very reputable people, synchronicity still faces criticism. Popper, for example, as Grattan-Guinness puts it, maintains that a lot of ideas, like synchronicity, take the status of unfalsifiable theories. He outlines in the chapter (*Conjectures and Refutations* ch. 8, London 1963) some of the difficulties in dealing with unfalsifiable theories, more particularly when many of those theories compete. For example, determinism, or solipsism versus realism, creates problems. Such problems can arise especially with those who doubt the theory of the synchronicity. It is difficult because some might also find the theory of 'unfalsifiable' limited.

Designed by Supernaturals

In my understanding, the theory of synchronicity is based on natural law, although some might also deny the existence of natural law. Hardy quoted Archbishop William Temple as saying, "When I pray, coincidences happen; when I don't, they don't."[66] Sir Arthur Conan Doyle in *The New Revelation* (1918) was originally very sceptical about psychic phenomena, but was gradually converted to an acceptance of them; during the First World War he had come to believe that they were "Something really tremendous, a breaking down of the walls between two worlds."[67] From then until his death he was deeply involved in psychical research. Conan Doyle also stated, as Inglis puts it, that there is "Some beneficent force outside ourselves, which tries to help us where it can. The old belief in guardian angels was not only attractive, he thought, but has in it, I believe, a real basis of truth or was it that the subliminal self has the ability to learn and convey to the mind that which our own known senses are unable to apprehend?"[68]

I share the same view. I believe there are some external forces, be it a guardian angel or God himself. The Mission England Praise No. 172 has these words: "O speak, and make me listen, Thou guardian of my soul. O guide me, call me, draw me, uphold me to the end."

James William (1842-1910) confessed that "The Creator has externally intended this department of nature to remain baffling, to prompt our curiosities and hopes and suspicions all in equal measure."[69] This applies to telepathy as well, as we shall see.

Bibliography

1. Holroyd S., *Psi and The Consciousness Explosion*, p. 191-2, The Bodley Head, London, Sydney, Toronto, 1977.
2. Ibid p. 192.
3. Koestler, A., *The Roots of Coincidence*, p.105, Hutchinson & Co (Publishers) Ltd, London, 1972.
4. Koestler, A., *The Act of Creation*, p. 101, Hutchinson, London, 1964.
5. Ibid p. 78.
6. Holroyd, S., op. cit. p. 193.
7. Inglis, B., *Coincidence; A Matter of Chance or Synchronicity?*, p. 18, by Hutchinson, London, 1990.
8. Ibid p. 13.
9. Ibid p. 22.
10. Ibid p. 17.
11. Baugham, A., *Incredible Coincidence*, p. 13.
12. Ibid p. 13.
13. Ibid p. 12.
14. Heywood, R., *The Sixth Sense*, p. 9, Corgi Books, London, 1981.
15. Ibid p. 10.
16. Lancaster, B., *Mind, Brain and Human Potential*, p. 36, Element, Shaftesbury, Dorset, Rockport, Massachusetts, 1992.
17. Ibid p. 37.
18. Ibid p. 37.
19. Ibid p. 37.
20. Ibid p. 37.

21. Ibid p.38.
22. Hardy, A. et al., *The Challenge of Chance*, p.177, by Hutchinson, London, 1973.
23. Ibid p. 177.
24. Jung, C.G., *The Structure & Dynamic of the Psyche*, vol. 8, p. 505, Routledge & Kegan Paul, London & Henley, 1977.
25. Beloff, J., Book Review: The Challenge of Chance p. 319-20, *SRP Journal*, March 1974.
26. Inglis, B., *Coincidence: A Matter of Chance or Synchronicity?*, p. 79, Hutchinson, London, 1990.
27. Ibid p. 79.
28. Ibid p. 80.
29. Jung, C.G., *Synchronicity*, p. 9, Routledge & Kegan Paul, London, 1955.
30. Jung, C.G., *The Structure & Dynamics of the Psyche*, vol. 8, p. 423, Routledge & Kegan Paul, London, 1977.
31. Jung, C.G., *Synchronicity*, p. 9.
32. Ibid p. 20-1.
33. Ibid p. 27.
34. Ibid p. 28.
35. Ibid p. 28.
36. Jung, C.G., *The Structure & Dynamics of the Psyche*, p. 441
37. Inglis,B., *The Unknown Quest*, p. 172, Chatto & Windus, London, 1987.
38. Ibid p. 172.
39. Beloff, J., *Journal of SPR*, vol. 49, No. 773, September 1977, p. 575. *Psi Phenomena. Causal Versus Acausal Interpretation.*
40. Hurkos, P., *Psychic*, p. 18, Wheaton & Co. Ltd., Great Britain, 1961/62
41. Hearne, K., *Visions of the Future*, p 103-4, The Aquarian Press, London, 1989.
42. Inglis, B., *The Unknown Quest*, op. cit. p. 171.
43. Jung, C.G., *Synchronicity*, op. cit. p. 103.
44. Ibid p. 103-4.
45. Ibid p. 103.

SYNCHRONICITY

46. Ibid p. 101.
47. Ibid p. 106.
48. Ibid p. 106.
49. Ibid p. 107.
50 Arkinson, R.L. et al., *An Introduction to Psychology*, p. 13, Harcourt Brace Jovanovich, London, Sydney, Toronto, USA, 1985.
51. Jung, C. G., *Synchronicity*, p. 107.
52. Ibid p. 107.
53. Ibid p. 107.
54. Ibid p. 108.
55. Puharich, A., *Beyond Telepathy*, p. 21, Pan Books, London, 1962.
56. Ullman, M. et al., *Dream Telepathy*, p. 23, McFarland & Co Inc. Publishers, Jefferson, North Carolina & London, 1989.
57. Hugh, L., Cayce et al., *Dreams, the Language of the Unconscious*, p. 37, Virginia Beach, Va: A.R.E. Press, 1962.
58. Watson, L., *Earthworks*, p. 30, Hodder & Stoughton, London, 1986.
59. Combs A. et al., "Synchronicity", *Science, Myth and the Trickster* – p. 1, Floris Books, U.S., 1990.
60. Guinness, I.G., "What are Coincidences?", *Journal, SPR*, December 1978, p. 950.
61. Ullman, M. et al., op. cit. p. 26.
62. Ibid p. 26.
63. Ibid p. 26.
64. Lancaster, B., *Mind, Brain and Human Potential*, op. cit. p. 39.
65. Jung, C.G., *Synchronicity*, p. 123 op. cit.
66. Hardy, A., "The Challenge of Chance", p. 111, op. cit.
67. Inglis, B., *The Paranormal: An Encyclopedia of Psychic Phenomena*, p. 289.
68. Inglis, B., "Coincidence: A Matter of Chance – Or Synchronicity", p. 53, op. cit.
69. Inglis, B., The Paranormal: *Encyclopaedia*, op. cit., p. 300.

CHAPTER 6

Telepathy and Clairvoyance

Most of us have stories to tell about various incidents which happen to us in a miraculous way; and we find it difficult to convince people that they are factual. Some people might believe us when we relate the story, but only if they know us very well and not merely know us, but trust us enough.

Equally parapsychology has the problem of subjectivity, since it is related to moral values or moral judgements. However, be it subjective or not, whatever we experience turns out to be a reality. There is still in parapsychology the problem of verification. Telepathy and clairvoyance tend in most cases to be an explanation of feeling. As such, some tend to regard extra-sensory-perception as illogical.

ESP Associated to Emotion

Extra-sensory-perception is equated to the theory of emotivism, that is the theory that ethical statements are expressions of feeling. For example, if something is labelled right or wrong, or good or bad, it is because it is thought to be an action of a certain type. This in itself seems to be important to Ayer in his book *Language, Truth and Logic*. He contended that what seems to be an ethical judgement is very often a factual classification; by which a certain moral attitude on the part of the speaker is habitually aroused.

Ayer was of the opinion that statements of value are simply expressions of emotion which can be neither true nor false.

Both the subjectivists and the Utilitarian philosophers believed that value statements could be translated. Ayer, however, believed that the validity of ethical judgements must be regarded as 'absolute' or 'intrinsic', and not empirically calculable. To claim empirical knowledge of things which are subjective seems to have no logical basis to positivist philosophers. Therefore, to demand a priori proof of the existence of the objects which are not immediately 'given' could sound illegitimate to the ears of some. Ayer holds that "Unless they are metaphysical objects, the occurrence of certain sense-experiences will itself constitute the only proof of their existence which is requisite or obtainable; and the question whether the appropriate sense-experiences do or do not occur in the relevant circumstances is one that must be decided in actual practice, and not by any a priori argumentation."[1]

Ayer has attributed this to the problem of perception. A.G. Moore, a Cambridge philosopher, argued that if ethical statements were simply statements about the speaker's feelings, then it would be impossible to argue about questions of value. This principle of verification is based on the assumption that the propositions of logic and mathematics are necessarily true statements, i.e. Wittgenstein suggested that these statements, if they are true or mathematical, should be regarded as 'tautologies'. It is the contention of logical positivism that every significant proposition must be analytical. Equally, all analytical propositions belong to a formal logic.

To me, statements about dreams, mysticism, telepathy etc are in themselves analytical. They are analytical because they are experiential. No one can invent them. A lady from Bath, who was a missionary in Malawi, is very concerned that I write a fictional book. Sometimes she gives me a title and I keep it in my diary. But in the end I don't use it simply because what I write is solely that which I have experienced. To write fiction would seem to be inverting the objects. Perhaps the time has not yet come. To this end what I write carries an element of a priori. If the principle of verification deals with truth, then one could argue that ESP is based on fact. This is then equally true of dream telepathy and clairvoyance. I have mentioned somewhere that I don't have much experience of this subject, but since I have experienced it once or twice, I felt compelled to write on telepathy and clairvoyance. But I do experience telepathy during the day, though not in a dream.

ESP as Mysteries

All the same, ESP could be equated to religion. Alister Hardy in his collaborative book, *The Challenge of Chance*, has the same contention. Thus he writes "The influence which religious people feel when they say they are in touch with what seems to them to be some transcendental element – a power that affects their lives, whether they call it God or not, may be something within the same field as extra-sensory telepathic communication."[2] But Hardy thinks it is 'premature' to try to 'speculate' what these things really are. Thus Hardy categorizes them as mysteries, a belief I tend to share.

These religious experiences are regarded as something which is inexpressible. Thus, in 1 Timothy 3 v. 16, Paul observes, "and great beyond all question is the mystery of our religion."[3] Some regard such religious experiences as having nothing to do with morality. William James, in quoting M. Taine, says: "Whether facts be moral or physical, it makes no matter."[4] James gives the example of Fox, the founder of the Quaker religion, that "everyone who confronted him personally from Oliver Cromwell down to County Magistrates and jailers, seems to have acknowledged his superior power."[5] For this reason James comments that "personal religion will prove itself more fundamental than either theology or ecclesiasticist"[6] James gives an example of Job when he cried, "Though he slay me, yet will I trust in him."

Religion, says James, is a new dimension of emotion. Kant,

who condemned transcendent metaphysics, but on different grounds, believed that "the human understanding was so constituted that it lost itself in contradictions when it ventured out beyond the limits of possible experience and attempted to deal with things in themselves."[7] For this reason Kant made the impossibility of transcendental metaphysics not, as we do, a matter of logic, but a matter of fact. Kant asserted "not that our minds could not conceivably have had the power of penetrating beyond the phenomenal world, but merely that they were in fact devoid of it."[8] Ayer concludes that this leads to the question: "If it is possible to know only what lies within the bounds of sense-experience."[9] He goes on to say, "The author can be justified in asserting that real things do exist beyond, and how he can tell what are the boundaries beyond which the human understanding may not venture, unless he succeeds in passing them himself."[10] I would have loved to continue with this argument, but doing so would seem to deviate in our argument, causing us to concentrate wholly on religion whereas this chapter mainly discusses telepathy.

James regards hallucination as the most profound proof of reality. To elaborate on this a little further, he says, "It is as if there were in the human consciousness a sense of reality, a feeling of objective presence, a perception of what we might call 'Something there'."[11] James gives his own experience, which took place in 1884. He had a vivid hallucination of being grasped by the arm. He got up and searched the room. The sense of presence came again the next night. He didn't recognise it by any ordinary sense and yet there was a horribly pleasant 'sensation' connected with it.

Telepathy Defined

What then is telepathy? I would define telepathy by quoting Ullman et al., famous American writers in parapsychology. In their book, *Dream Telepathy*, they define telepathy as "fellow-feeling at a distance, including not only thought transference between distant persons but also emotional and less definable impressions."[12] This definition was first coined by F.W.H. Myers, a famous classical scholar and an inspector of schools, in 1882. Empson, in his book, *Sleep And Dreaming*, states that "individuals somehow become aware of facts which were inaccessible to their senses (clairvoyance), or had a vision of the future (precognition), or they received a communication from another person with whom there was no physical contact (telepathy)".[13] Soal et al. state that "experimentally it has proved extremely difficult to discriminate between telepathy and clairvoyance."[14]

Telepathy, as I understand it, is one of the extra-sensory-perceptions, except that telepathy and clairvoyance were used long before the term 'extra-sensory-perception' was wholly accepted. Telepathy, as Rhine, quoting from Frederic W.H. Myers, puts it, was originally defined as "a direct mind-to-mind contact, not involving any physical intermediation."[15] In other words, it is the communication of mind to mind without really affecting the five senses we have.

Perhaps it is feasible to see what Freud had to say on the subject. He never really believed in telepathic dreams, since he did not have one himself. But he was later intrigued by the possibility of their existence after hearing a case "in which his psychoanalytic theories seemed to demonstrate that telepathy occurring in dreams is distorted in much the same way as material in ordinary dreams."[16] A middle-aged man wrote that he had dreamed vividly of his wife giving birth to twins. Soon after, he received a telegram from his daughter's husband with the news that his daughter had given birth to twins on the same night as his dream. At first the couple had expected one child as confirmed by their doctor, but in the end the couple had twins, perhaps to fulfil the dream.

This dream left a remarkable impression on Freud. What particularly impressed him was the substitution in the dream of the man's wife for the daughter. "Because the dreamer's erotic feelings towards his daughter would be expressed from conscious thought, the wife would be substituted for the daughter to be acceptable to the dreamer's conscious."[17] Freud gave an example, as Ullman et al. put it, "It is evident how the message, with the help of a lurking repressed wish, becomes remodelled into a wish fulfilment."[18] To this end the tracing of telepathic dreams made Freud believe that it is an "incontestable fact that sleep creates favourable conditions for telepathy." This view was, as Ullman asserts, upheld by surveys of spontaneous cases of ESP. Freud then later wrote that telepathy "may be the original archaic method by which individuals understood one another, and which has been pushed into the background in the course of phylogenetic (evolutionary) development by the better method of communication by means of signs apprehended by the sense organs. But such older methods may have persisted in the background, and may still manifest under certain conditions..."[19]

Freud's contemporary, psychiatrist and parapsychologist Dr. Jule Eisenburd said, as quoted by Ullman et al., "One of the greatest advances – to my mind the greatest – in the study of telepathy and allied phenomena occurred when Freud made the simple observation that psychoanalysis was capable of unmasking a telepathic event which otherwise could not be recognised as such."[20]

Jung, on the other hand, was of the contention that "crisis telepathy is often not immediate in time – the experience occurring either just before or after an event – is supported by spontaneous cases collected by parapsychologists."[21] Freud noted that "telepathic dreams often appear in the dreamer's consciousness later than the event, after a so-called latency period"; but he categorically rejected the verified observation that "such dreams often occurred just before the event."[22] The precognitive element in dreams increased doubt in Freud's mind, to the extent that he declared, when delivering lectures, that clairvoyance cases go wrong, or perhaps that they happen, because of the unconscious memory. Jung had no doubts since he himself had experienced prophetic dreams. Thus he wrote, as Ullman et al. put it, "In all these cases, whether it is a question of spatial or temporal ESP, we find a simultaneity of the normal ordinary state with another state or experience which is not causally derivable from it, and whose objective existence can only be verified afterwards."[23]

Telepathy Related to Other ESP

I think these things overlap. What we may call psychic experience, dreams, precognition or synchronicity, might turn out to be a form of telepathy. I could refer to the dream I had about my brother, as shown in *The Usefulness of Dreams: An African Perspective*. I need not repeat the dream. But whilst I was in the middle of that dream, my brother rang me from home in Malawi. He had never rung me before since he left Britain. It was the first time he had rung me. This left a remarkable impression on me. Prior to this I could not accept anything in the name of telepathy. I doubted whether things do happen. I would sometimes associate it with the work of the devil, just coming to deceive us. As for clairvoyance, I associated it with magic. Yet again dream clairvoyance happened to me when I was a little girl, when I lost 10s. and knew where it was in a dream.

Brain Relationship or What

Concerning clairvoyance, my message in this chapter is concerned with other people's experiences. But with telepathy happening to me frequently during the day, I have come to believe that it is the work of a guardian angel. There must be an outside agency monitoring our day-to-day activities. There are times when I tend to think these extra-sensory perceptions are associated with brain relationships. It's easy to reason like this when it happens to the people within the same family or of the same clan. I related another example in *The Usefulness of Dreams*. A friend of mine used to live in Liverpool and left to settle in London. He didn't get in touch with me for quite a long time after he left. As it happened, I was supposed to attend a two-day seminar in London. I did not book a hotel. The lady who was organising the seminar rang me to find out if I was going. I said 'yes' in good faith. I told my line manager about it and he said I should not go. He did not want me to sleep in the streets. But I told him the Lord was going to provide something.

When I went to my house after work, I tried to ring a number of people to see if they could provide me with my friend's telephone number, but nobody seemed to have it. It was by then 10.00 p.m., and I feared I was going to miss the 6 a.m. train. So I decided to go to bed. As I was entering my bedroom, the telephone rang and it was my friend. I could not believe it. However, I asked him if he could book a hotel for me. He told me just to hold on to the telephone; he told the family he was staying with, and they decided to invite me to stay in their house for two days. In this case there was no brain relationship, since my friend is British and I am an African. I regarded this as both psychic and telepathic. It was psychic in the sense that I had thought about him while at work as someone to help me with the hotel bookings, and telepathy in the sense he was to ring me when I was trying to find his phone number.

Jung, commenting on this, wrote: "Therefore they are recognised at first only as psychic entities and are conceived as such, with the same right with which we base the physical phenomena of immediate perception on Euclidean space. Only when it comes to explaining psychic phenomena of a minimal degree of clarity are we driven to assume that archetypes must have a non-psychic aspect. Grounds for such a conclusion are supplied by the phenomena of synchronicity, which are associated with the activity of unconscious operations and have hitherto been regarded, or repudiated, as 'telepathy,' etc." Jung added that no unbiased observer can deny their existence. And that "Resistance to the recognition of such facts rests principally on the repugnance people feel for allegedly supernatural faculty tacked on to psychic, like clairvoyance."

With the two examples given above, the dreams concerning my brother and the trip to London, I cannot wholly say there is a brain relationship. I would be inclined to agree if it was only from family to family viz-a-viz the dream concerning my brother. But one finds it hard when a puzzle involves someone from outside the family, as in the case of Brian Roughborne (my friend). However, that there is a brain relationship cannot be ruled out.

Telepathic Dream by Sandra Edwards

A colleague at work, Sandra Edwards, shared with me her own dream experience which relates to telepathy. She writes in her own words:

"I have a pen-friend in Florida, United States. He is a doctor. Whenever I wrote to him and didn't receive a reply I didn't worry, because he is a busy man. However, one day a strange feeling came over me, my head hurt. Though it was not like having a headache, it was different. My pen-friend had been involved in a car crash on his way home from work. He was hurt badly, having to stay in hospital for months. When he was in hospital, he told me he thought of me constantly. (He was unable to write because his hands were hurt). I believe through telepathic thoughts he was telling me something was wrong."

All these stories – or mysteries I would rather call them – have not been exaggerated. I trust Sandra, and whatever she tells me I believe it, because of what she is. She has an admirable character.

Two Friends Dreaming at the Same Time of the Same Thing

A good example is that given by Holroyd in his book, *Dream World*. He records Dr. Adele Gleason's dream. She dreamed that she was in a deserted spot in the midst of very dark woods. She was suddenly terribly afraid that a man she knew well, John R. Joslyn, might arrive unexpectedly and shake the tree next to her, causing the leaves to fall and burst into flames. She got up and recorded the time and Joslyn's initials. Upon meeting him, she told him of the dream she had had on the previous Tuesday night.

Joslyn told her that he also had had a dream the same night she noted. He cited his first, saying, "I dreamed that I was walking at night in a remote spot where I sometimes go shooting. Soon I saw in the bushes, about 12 yards from the road, one of my woman friends apparently paralyzed with fear of something that I did not see, rooted to the spot by the feeling of imminent danger. I came to her and shook the bush, upon which the leaves that fell from it burst into flames."[24] The two dreams had occurred at the same time.

Ghostly Connection Between Men and Animals

Holroyd gives another example of an interesting telepathic dream experienced by the novelist Rider Haggard, this time between a human and an animal, which is very interesting and very unusual. He dreamt that a dog was lying on its side in rough growth on the edge of water. It was clearly in pain and seemed to be struggling to speak to him. "My own personality," he states, "in some mysterious way seemed to me to be rising from the body of the dog, which I knew quite surely to be Bob and no other.[25] In my vision the dog was trying to speak to me in words, and failing, transmitted to my mind in an unidentified fashion the knowledge that it was dying. Then everything vanished and I woke to hear my wife asking why on earth I was making those horrible and weird noises."

Holroyd also reports that the novelist shared his dream with five people the following morning. Later it was discovered the dog had gone missing. They all remembered the dream. Four days later the body of the dog was found against the weir in a nearby river. It was reported that the dog was hit by a train at 11 o'clock the previous Saturday night. Holroyd says "it was not possible to ascertain the precise moment of death, but it could well have coincided with Haggard's dream, which occurred at one o'clock in the morning about two hours after the accident."[26]

The novelist, as Holroyd reports, concluded by saying: "I cannot venture to speak further than to say that... it does seem to suggest that there is a more intimate ghostly connection between all members of the animal world, including men, than has hitherto been believed, at any rate by Western people; that they may be, in short, all of them different manifestations of some central, informing life, though inhabiting the universe in such various shapes"[27].

I am inclined to believe that in dream telepathy angelic powers play a great part. It is not only the work of the mind, nor are they coincidences, but angelic powers do send messages to us to tell us what is happening at the other end. Each individual, I believe, does have a guardian spirit to take care of him or her. Let us consider the novelist's account above. It seems to me that he loved his dog very much; therefore, the spirits or the ghost, as he puts it himself, had to inform him what was happening to his dog.

A lot of scientists and rationalists regard dream telepathy or clairvoyance as nonsensical. They want something which is observable. Some of us have learned to believe that dream telepathy, clairvoyance, ordinary dreams etc. are not just implausible. They are based on facts. Brian Inglis wrote in the *Guardian* in 1987, "Even hundreds and hundreds of rationalists cannot deny the powerfulness of dreams."[28]

Time Counts Telepathing

Dain, as Holroyd has shown in his book, *Dream Worlds*, conducted his experiments in the early morning hours and participated in them himself, sometimes as sender and sometimes as receiver. The material to be transmitted was a coloured geometric shape, selected at random from a pile of envelopes containing various coloured shapes. The sender concentrated on the image with the object of projecting it into the dream consciousness of the receiver. Sender and receiver were sometimes located as far as four miles apart. On one occasion Dain concentrated on a red equilateral triangle on a black background. After a few minutes of concentration, he felt that he had been successful in transmitting the image, and he willed the receiver to wake up. The time he began the experiment was 6.30 a.m.

The receiver later reported that he had awakened at 6.30 a.m. He remembers a dream involving music and soldiers. Suddenly in the midst of the soldiers, appeared "a three-cornered, glaring red fir tree... It pushes through the whole... and remains unmoved for seconds amid all the former dream contents. It is not a fir tree out of nature but such as one finds in children's primers, the trunk is black, colour distinct, while all the other dream contents are of a colourless gray. In other words, the shape of a red equilateral triangle with a black background interpreted his ongoing dream at the time Dain was attempting to project such a pattern."[29]

Perhaps a more touching telepathic dream is the one by Sir John Drummond Hay, a distinguished figure in the British diplomatic service, who heard his daughter-in-law's cry in a dream. Sir John Drummond sent his report signed by three other witnesses. Here is the full story as quoted by Stevens in his book, *The Mystery of Dreams*, 1950.

"In the year 1879 my son Robert Drummond Hay resided at Mogodor with his family, where he was at the time Consul. It was the month of February. I had lately received good accounts of my son and his family; I was also in perfect health. About one a.m. (I forget the exact day in February) whilst sleeping soundly (at Tangier), I was awakened by distinctly hearing the voice of my daughter-in-law, who was with her husband at Mogodar, saying in a clear but distressed tone of voice, "Oh, I wish papa only knew that Robert is ill." There was a night lamp in the room, but there was no one except my wife, sleeping quietly in bed. I listened for some seconds, expecting to hear footsteps outside, but complete stillness prevailed, so I lay down again, thanking God that the voice which woke me was hallucination. I had hardly closed my eyes when I heard the same voice and words, upon which I woke Lady Drummond Hay and told her what had occurred, and got up and went into my study, adjoining the bedroom, and noted it in my diary. Next morning I related what had happened to my daughter, saying that, though I did not believe in dreams, I felt anxious for tidings from Mogodar. That port, as you will see on the map, is about three hundred miles south of Tangier. A few days after this incident a letter arrived from my daughter-in-law, Mrs R. Drummond Hay, telling us that my son was seriously ill with typhoid fever and mentioning the night during which he had been delirious. Much struck by the coincidence that it was the same night I had heard her voice, I wrote to tell her what had happened. She replied by the following post ... that in her distress at seeing her husband so dangerously ill, and from being alone in a distant land, she had made use of the precise words which had startled me from sleep, and had repeated them. As it may be of interest to you to receive a corroboration of what I have related from the persons I have mentioned, who happened to be with me at this date, they also sign to affirm the accuracy of all I have related.[30]

signed:
J.H. Drummond Hay
Annette Drummond Hay
Euphemia Drummond Hay
Alice Drummond Hay.   Sept 16 1889

Telepathy and synchronicity tend to overlap, especially when you think of telephoning, as has already been discussed. Thus Combs et al. assert, "Other examples of meaningful coincidences which may be explained by the existence of morphic fields are more common but less dramatic. They include relatively frequent situations in which two or more persons are thinking of doing things at the same time, but with no knowledge of each other."[31] I rang a girl in the office the other day. Her friend received my telephone call while she herself was on the phone trying to ring me, only to receive the engaged tone. The other girl told me to hold. The one I was ringing got fed up because my telephone was engaged. She put the receiver down. She was told, "Mary is

136

on the phone for you", whereupon she said "That's the one I was ringing but her telephone was engaged." So my telephone was engaged because I was ringing her. She told me when she spoke to me. Thus, Combs et al. state, "Both of you were contemplating the conversation prior to the call or you find yourself thinking something just when a person nearby starts to talk about it as if to spare you the trouble."[32] They add that "In instances such as these, synchronicity may overlap with what we normally think of as telepathy."[33]

These strange powers will continue to exist forever. Even if science continues to ignore them, they would continue to appear or to happen since, in my belief, God alone has ordained them. I was fascinated by the following story of an event which happened in 1610. John Donne, who was a metaphysical poet, went to France on a diplomatic tour. His wife was by then pregnant. Whilst there, Donne found himself in an ecstatic mood, as Clarkes puts it in his book, *World of Strange Powers*. Donne said to Sir Robert Drury, the British Ambassador to France, "I have seen a dreadful vision since I saw you: I have seen my dear wife pass twice by me through this room, with her hair hanging about her shoulders and a dead child in her arms..."[34] The ambassador suggested it was perhaps "the result of some melancholy dream", but Donne insisted it was a vision. They sent a messenger to England to check on Donne's wife. The messenger reported that "he found and left Mrs Donne very sad and sick in her bed; and that after a long and dangerous labour, she had been delivered of a dead child... And upon examination, the abortion proved to be on the same day, at about the very hour, that Donne affirmed he saw her pass by him in his chamber."[35]

It is also believed that telepathy happens in twins. This incident happened in 1984. It is again told by Clarkes. Christine Young of Mexborough in South Yorkshire reported feeling pain. She experienced the very same pain which her twin sister Carol experienced while in labour. Her sister was having a baby boy. It seems as if many people, as Clarkes puts it, "believe that they can receive the thought of members of their family, often over considerable distances."[36] This has already been discussed earlier on.

Coincidences in Animals As Well

For example, Mr E. Hopkins, who runs his own drama school, told me a story of their cat which got lost and they forgot about it. One day they were talking about that cat, remembering how lovely it was and how they were missing it. Whilst in the middle of the conversation, the cat just came on the scene from nowhere. This is also supported by Arthur Clarke. In his book, *World of Strange Powers*, he tells of other, allegedly psychic pets which came under Rhine's scrutiny, including a dog called Chris from Rhode Island who had a talent for predicting the next day's winners at Narragansett, and Sugar, a cat who travelled from California to Oklahoma."[37]

Stories of this kind are very common in my country, Malawi. If a dog or a cow goes missing, we don't worry because everyone knows it will eventually come back, even if it takes two weeks or a month. It sometimes happens that the people concerned go to look for their cow and give up after a week; then it arrives on its own. One of our cows went missing when I was young. My father and some boys looked for it and then gave up. After two weeks it came back on its own. What normally happens is that it will go to mix with other cows in another village; then one day it will just run away from them and work out its way home. As for a dog, it can go as far as Mozambique, one of the neighbouring countries, and come back after some time. It is really strange that after one has forgotten it, it appears upon one member of the family mentioning it.

Slips of the Tongue

Another form of coincidence could be seen in 'Freudian' slips of the tongue. These are hidden thoughts in us and they come out of their own accord unknowingly, and can become a puzzle even to the person who actually utters the words. Their prediction may be sometimes good or sometimes bad. I don't know how it happens that in some cases there are things I want to keep secret or to myself, yet I find myself saying them unconsciously and later come to my senses. This agrees with what Combs et al. wrote: "Freud's notion of parapraxes refers to the false but embarrassing acts commonly called Freudian slips. They often reveal hidden truths about our makeup, showing the human bumbler behind the smooth and ordered facade we project to others."[38]

Combs et al. give an example provided by one of the authors who attended a lecture given by an ageing professor. The professor was giving a highly creative talk on the meaning of Ingmar Bergman's film, "Wild Strawberries". The audience were surprised on hearing the professor when he exclaimed, "See: as I grow older my procreative powers – excuse me – my creative powers, grow greater and greater."[39] The professor emphasised that added notion. Combs et al. then state: "A slip of the tongue may reveal its meaning in terms of unconscious psychological or emotional needs."[40] They comment that "This slip, which without knowledge of psychology we would take simply as nonsensical, is not difficult to understand in terms of the speaker's fear of the loss of sexual potency as he approaches old age. Such slips unveil a connection between the world of emotions. Like parapraxes, synchronistic events also connect different worlds: the world of everyday reality with the world of the mythic realms of the unconscious."[41]

It also sometimes happens that you tell your friends something in a joke and it later happens. I will mention the names of people involved in the following story to avoid the issue of it being subjective. I was interested in writing a book about HIV when it had just started, especially in dealing with the suggestion that it originated in Africa. I wanted to refute that myth. To this end I started collecting material for the book. We were one day chatting, four of us, Angela Kafumba, Charles Kafumba, Brian Roughbourne and myself. During this conversation I myself said

I was going to write a book on HIV and Brian said no, I could not write because I am not a nurse qualified to write on HIV. I argued that one does not need to be a nurse for such a task. It all depends, according to one's interest. Charles supported me. But Brian insisted that I needed to have an authority in order to do that. I replied: "I will in future get a job on HIV/AIDS, and I will then have the authority." Angela asked whether I meant it and I said "Yes, I will get a job." This was 1989.

After a year in 1990 I got a job with the Liverpool City Council on HIV/AIDS. How I got it is also very interesting. I strongly believe it was to fulfil what I had said a year before. Two of us went for an interview for this post. The job was given to the other lady, who came from London. She had computer skills whilst I myself did not. I was devastated and did not know what to do, because I thought it was truly my job as I had predicted it a year ago. But since we all did well at the interview, I was still taken and given a different job in Community Care. I was truly disappointed. How could I go wrong in my prediction? The story does not end there. My colleague could not start the job in time since she had just had a baby. For this reason she asked if she could start work six weeks later. After all, she had to give notice at her old job. I myself was then asked to do the HIV job. Honestly I was not surprised, for I was strongly convinced that it was my job. The Social Services Directorate wanted someone to fill the HIV post as soon as possible. So they had to take me, since I was already working with them. But then, having said this, I don't know what made me say I was going to work in the HIV field. Besides, I was not applying for any jobs. When my colleague came she was asked to work on Learning Difficulties. My line manager, Phil Purvis, said he was going to do Community Care himself.

Angela Kafumba was greatly puzzled to hear that I had got this HIV post. She said I knew about the job. But how could I know about it as early as 1989, and it was in May 1990 when I got the job? I was more puzzled than Angela. Brian Roughborne was less puzzled since this kind of thing does happen to him. Equally I don't know whether I could connect this with a Freudian slip of the tongue. It follows, then, that talking about the future is also a kind of synchronistic happening or telepathy. It was as if some angel had sent some kind of signal to me.

Jung's notion of synchronicity, as Combs et al. observed, is based on the idea that when the unconscious mind is stimulated powerfully in one direction there is a corresponding lowering of mental energy elsewhere. This frees up psychoid or undifferentiated levels of mind. This primitive level is free of the ordinary restraints which separate the mind from connections with the external world. When such connections are made, they are made in the form of synchronistic events."[42]

Rhine was impressed with these strange happenings and he is the one who categorized them as ESP. He went to the extent of using Zenner cards to test their validity. He marked them with five symbols, for example a star, a cross, a square, a circle and wavy lines. Each symbol was marked on five cards so he ended up having 25 cards in the pack. The experimenter would look at those cards one by one and the guesser would name them. The guesser would only be said to have passed if he named all five cards correctly. "But whatever he called, he should score an average of five by chance alone. Anything better might indicate that there was a hidden power involved: the faculty of ESP."[43]

In 1931 Rhine tested a volunteer economics student, Adam Linzmayer. What Rhine did was to place nine cards face down and, to Rhine's amazement, Linzmayer described all the symbols correctly. But later Linzmayer provided poor results. Rhine later, in collaboration with J. Gaither Prant, tested Hubert Pearce, a divinity student. Prant tested Hubert and he scored 9 out 25 cards. Rhine tested him as well and he scored 25 out of 25. It seemed as if Hubert was psychic. He continued winning, but when he left the Duke Laboratory and started his ministerial work, his powers seemed to have deserted him in a similar manner to Linzmayer.

Arthur Clarke then stated that "Proof of the existence of ESP seemed to be within reach. Our plan has been to try to catch what looks like ESP and, gradually improving the safeguards as we go, bring the phenomenon, if possible, up to the point where there can be no question about the interpretation of the results."[44]

Rhine was Criticised

Rhine's attempts to further the acceptance of ESP research as a branch of science were criticised by both colleagues and scientists and psychologists throughout America. Rhine faced hostility from many of the people who surrounded him. As Clarke had put it, "It was not known whether the good scores were a result of an agency other than ESP."[45] Mark Hansel, at the time Professor of Psychology at the University of Wales, a formidable analyst of claims for ESP, maintained it to be so. Unlike others, he thought of examining the work of the parapsychologists. He was then compelled to say "If ESP is merely an artifact, it is then important to understand how conventional experimental methods can yield results leading to erroneous conclusions."[46]

Given the findings discussed above, Rhine invited Hansel to visit him, and Hansel did so in 1960. The journey was specifically to examine Rhine's work. Hansel found that the results at Duke Campus had a fatal flaw. He performed this in a true British way. Hansel went there mainly to observe and see what conclusion he would come to. The tests which Hansel examined critically were those which Pratt conducted with Hubert Pearce, the divinity student. Pearce sat in a small room in the university library whilst Pratt conducted the experiments from a building 100 yards away. The tests went like this, as Clarke has put it: "Pratt would shuffle and cut a pack of ESP cards, and put it face down on the table. At the appointed moment, he would start to work through each pack, Pratt would wait for five minutes and then begin another 'run' with different cards. At the end of a test he would turn each card face-up, record the order in which they had been dealt, and send a copy of his list to Rhine. Meanwhile Pearce, 100 yards away in his library cubicle, finalised his score sheet. Later the results would be compared."[47]

The experiments seemed perfectly good to Pratt and Rhine, but not to Hansel, who scrutinised them in the British fashion. Hansel thought of performing the test himself. He asked a laboratory staff member, Wadhi, "to sit in a locked office and go through a pack of ESP cards just as Pratt had done."[48] Hansel went to sit in another office. It turned out that Hansel revealed to Saleh that he passed through the room and saw how the cards were arranged. Saleh's desk was sixteen feet from the door so that he was not able to see what Hansel was doing.

Some writers on this subject think that probably Pearce would leave the library and peep through a crack in the top of the door and copy the cards or memorise them; or else, since each experiment was properly timed, it might well be that Pearce got familiar with that timing and knew exactly which card Pratt was going to call.

However, Hansel's attack on Pratt's experiments was a blow to both Rhine and Pratt, "Since they were intended to provide conclusive proof of ESP and to shake the very foundation of science."[49] It was sad that Hubert Pearce died before Hansel's criticisms were made. However, another criticism arose from the fact that Rhine used home-made cards. In that respect some researchers thought, as Clarke puts it, that "these often made things easier, since the symbol on each one could often be detected by carefully studying its edge."[50] Also those Duke experiments failed to work in other places. Though Rhine was faced with all these criticisms, he continued to work until his death in 1980.

Dr. Samuel George Soal, the London University mathematician, like Rhine did a meticulous ESP experiment on a stage-mind reader, 'Frederic Marion'. "Marion's act was sensational. He could discover an object hidden in a cluttered room in seconds and unhesitatingly identify which of six boxes concealed a gold ring."[51] Soal believed that Marion was conditioned to read unconscious muscular signals through those involved in the experiment. Soal tried Rhine's cards and they did not work, which discouraged him. Rhine discovered this and wrote to Soal to check his results. However, Soal was to some extent discouraged. Later a new theory by a psychical researcher emerged and this gave Soal inspiration. The new theory suggested that there was a displacement effect, and this meant, as Clarke puts it, that "although the subject failed to identify the 'target' card, he was instead, calling either the previous one or the one that came directly after."[52] But when Soal went through the old score sheets in 1939, as Clarke states "he found to his gratified surprise that two sets of results showed striking 'displacement effects'."[53]

The subject of further experimentation was Basil Shackleton, a fashionable professional photographer, who claimed his psychic powers were at their best in the evening, especially after a drink or two, but who had failed to show any signs of telepathic ability; another subject was Mrs. Gloria Stewart, the wife of a consultant engineer from Richmond, Surrey. Soal's curiosity was aroused, and he decided to embark upon a new series of tests with Shackleton and Stewart. With his criticisms of the Duke University methods in mind, he devised a new and apparently stringent set of conditions under which the investigations were to be concluded, but did not want to be open to or have to welcome criticisms like those against Rhine.

He produced different cards from those of Rhine, and these he thought were easier to perceive. He used different kinds of animals. The experiments were conducted at Shackleton's studio and in a private house, in Richmond. The person to receive the symbols was called the percipient and the one to transmit them was called the agent. They sat in different rooms and were observed by an experimenter. The percipient would guess which card the agent was dealing and record the answer. The cards were examined at the end of 50 runs, "and Soal's random number tables were sent to a distinguished and unbiased professor at Cambridge. The results were higher than chance and this suggested that ESP existed. For example, Shackleton scored 1,101 out of 3,789 cards." As a result, the theory became a fact. The existence of the 'displacement effect' was established.

However, Soal was still criticised, especially with the telepathic tests he did with schoolboys. There is no room here to relate other tests which Soal did. But like Rhine, he also met with criticism. Mrs. Grett Albert, who acted as the agent, admitted to having peeped through a hole and seen Soal changing the figures on the sheet. Soal died in 1975. In *The Usefulness of Dreams* I referred to those dreams taken in the laboratory as 'artificial' and to private dreams as 'natural'. 'Natural' in the sense that no one has caused them to happen and they have not been induced. Those dreams I have regarded as been sent by God. In the same way I have regarded the use of cards in the laboratory as something which the experimenter would want to see happening. To this end this book is concerned with angelic guidance. It is a phenomenon which puzzles us and causes us to ask: "Why has it happened in this way?" Is it just accidental or chance?" In the final analysis you may find the answer is 'no', but still conclude that there must be some hidden power. To me this hidden power is nothing but God. However, this book is more about synchronicity. An example is provided by the following story.

On Monday morning at 6.10 a.m. I had a dream about a colleague, a Deputy Divisional Social Work Manager. By then I was writing a book on synchronicity, and the previous night I had been writing a chapter on telepathy and clairvoyance. The dream was about some problems about which I need not go into detail. But in the dream, my colleague came to collect me from work, and we went to a building. It was a multi-storey building. There were some people in the building, my line manager and two other men. I told my colleague I was going to the bank, and that I would come back to find her. I went and came back. Upon reaching the building, these other two men were coming down the stairs and one of them said: "Your friend has got problems." I said "She never told me." That was the end of the dream.

I went to my place of work on the same day as I had had the dream. I was still worried about her, and thought I might ring her. Round about 10.40 a.m. I rang the Royal Liverpool Hospital

Trust, where my colleague works, to enquire how she was getting on. I was disappointed to learn she was off work until Friday. I decided to drop her a letter so that she would find it when she came back to work. First of all, I went to make tea so that I could drink it while writing my friend's letter. On entering the office after making the cup of tea at about 10.45 a.m., to my amazement I found my colleague sitting in my chair. I shouted "a-a ...." in my language, "I have just rung your office, and they told me you were off until Friday." She said: "Yes, but I have come because I am going to Sefton General for interviews." I continued saying it wasn't really bad, it was about such-and-such a problem. I took her aside to a different office. I related the whole dream. She told me it was true that there were problems and she started relating the story to me. I interpreted the dream to mean telepathy or synchronicity, because I started at 9.30 am; wanting to ring her, but could not get to her. I was busy. Thus, I would not be wrong to interpret that at the time I had been wanting to ring her, she was already getting ready to come to see me.

The above is one of the examples which puzzle me. Such kinds of phenomena are natural in themselves. They are also similar to those in which people can, through ESP, tell where missing property is (clairvoyance). They do not perform magic; it just happens of its own accord. Perhaps this could be called intuition, as I conceive it, one of the basic functions of the psyche, namely, perception of the possibilities inherent in a situation.

Clairvoyance Defined

I have already defined clairvoyance in chapter 2, but here I shall attempt to show how it is related to intuitionism. Some have associated clairvoyance with intuitionism. Intuitionism is the apprehension of something as right at the particular moment you are seeing it. Jung, as Evans puts it in his book (1964) *Jung on Elementary Psychology*, has called intuitionism 'irrational'. He defines rational and irrational; for example "the rational group consists of the two functions, thinking and feeling. The ideal thinking is a rational reassurance. They hold rational values. That is differentiated thinking."[54]

The irrational group is comprised of the sensational type: the ideal perception is that you have an accurate perception of thinking; without additions or corrections. On the other hand, in intuition a person does not look at things as they are. He looks briefly at things as they are and makes off into an unconscious process at the end of which he/she will see something nobody else will see. To some extent intuitionism might be regarded as irrational on the basis that it is not based on facts, but on apprehension. Equally, some in the final analysis, might regret having called intuitionism irrational. I should think clairvoyance is very much connected to telepathy. Your mind is connected to the object wherever it is. Whether it involves perceiving or feeling, there is still an element of the mind involved in clairvoyance.

Given the facts above, one would be inclined to say clairvoyance is different from intuitionism, because it is based on fact or experiential happenings. An example is that given by Holroyd in his book, *Dream Worlds*. He gives a well-known tale of dream clairvoyance that solved a mystery in the Red Barn murder case. The case happened in 1927; Maria Marten, from Suffolk (England), ran away with Mr. Corder, who was a farmer. Corder became involved with another woman and decided to murder Maria. He did so and buried her under the floor of a barn. He then wrote a letter to Maria's parents that he and Maria had got married and were living happily together. In view of such a letter, nobody thought of a crime, so a year elapsed.

Maria's mother had a vivid dream in which she told things as they were. Acting upon that dream; the truth was revealed. Having presented a strong case for dream clairvoyance above, Holroyd asserts that "it is difficult to avoid the conclusion that some minds possess a faculty for 'seeing' objects and events paranormally, and that this sometimes operates through dreams."[55] I would accept clairvoyance as rational.

That some people do experience telepathy or clairvoyance cannot be denied. The stories people share with each other are not inverted or imagined. With this in mind, I am compelled to believe we all possess different gifts, as the Apostle Paul put it. "Now there are varieties of gifts, but the same Spirit; and there are varieties of service, but the same Lord; and there are varieties of working, but it is the same God who inspires them all in everyone. To each is given the manifestation of the Spirit for the common good. To one is given through the Spirit the utterance of Wisdom, and to another gifts of healing by the one Spirit, to another the working of miracles, to another prophecy, to another the ability to distinguish between spirits, to another various kinds of tongues, to another the interpretation of tongues. All these are inspired by one and same Spirit, who apportions to each one individually as he wills." 1 Corinthians 12 v.4f (RSV). Paul continues: "For just as the body is one and has many members, and all the members of the body, though many, are one body, so it is with Christ."

Bibliography

1. Ayer, A.J., *Language, Truth & Logic*, p. 46, Penguin Books Ltd, Harmondsworth, U.K., 1972.
2. Hardy, A. et al., *The Challenge of Chance*, p. 15, Hutchinson & Co (Publisher) Ltd, London, Melbourne, Sydney, Auckland, 1973.
3. 1 Timothy 3 v. 16 (RSV)
4. James, W., *The Varieties of Religious Experience*, p. 32, Collins, London, 1968/85.
5. Ibid p. 30.
6. Ibid p. 49.
7. Ayer, op. cit. p. 46.
8. Ayer, op. cit. p. 47.
9. Ayer, op. cit. p. 47.
10 Ayer, op. cit. p. 47.
11. James, W., op. cit. p. 73.

12. Ullman, M. et al., *Dream Telepathy*, p. 10, McFarland & Company Inc., Publishing. Jefferson, North Carolina & London, 1989.
13. Empson, J., *Sleep And Dreaming*, p. 124, Faber & Faber Ltd, London, 1989
14. Soal, S.G. et al., *Modern Experiments in Telepathy*, p. 8, Greenwood Press, New Haven, 1954.
15. Rhine, J.B., "New World of the Mind", p. 23, Faber and Faber, London, 1953.
16. Ullman, M. et al., op. cit p. 23.
17. Ibid p. 23.
18. Ibid p. 23.
19. Ibid p. 23.
20. Ibid p. 23.
21. Ibid p. 24.
22. Ullman, M. et al., op. cit p. 25.
23. Ibid p. 25
24. Holroyd, S., *Dream Worlds*, p. 105, Aldous Books, London, 1976.
25. Ibid p. 106.
26. Ibid p. 109.
27. Ibid p. 109.
28. Inglis, B., *The Guardian*, September 1987.
29. Holroyd, S., op cit p. 101-2
30. Stevens, W.O., *The Mystery of Dreams*, p. 64-5, George Allen & Unwin Ltd, London 1950.
31. Combs, A. et al., "Synchronicity" *Science, Myth & The Trickster*, p.25, Paragon House, N.Y., 1990.
32. Ibid p. 25.
33. Ibid p. 25.
34. Clarkes, A., *World of Strange Powers*, p. 128, by Guild Publishing, London, 1985.
35. Ibid p. 128.
36. Ibid p. 127.
37. Ibid p. 136.
38. Combs, A. et al., op. cit. p. 94.

39. Ibid p. 95.
40. Ibid p. 95.
41. Ibid p. 95.
42. Ibid p. 95.
43. Clarkes, A., op. cit p. 136.
44. Ibid p. 137.
45. Ibid p. 137.
46. Ibid p. 138.
47. Ibid p. 139.
48. Ibid p. 139.
49. Ibid p. 140.
50. Ibid p. 140.
51. Ibid p.140-1.
52. Clarkes, A., op. cit. p. 141.
53. Ibid p. 141.
54. Evans, R., *Jung on Elementary Psychology*, p. 140, Routledge & Kegan Paul, London, 1964.
55. Holroyd, S., *Dream Worlds*, p. 102, Aldous Books, London, 1976.

CHAPTER 7

Dreaming for the Future
and the Present

Among the different kinds of coincidences, dreams seem to be the greatest of all. Dreams have left a remarkable impression on me. I have always listened to the dreams of other people with great interest and dreams have always puzzled me. I have always maintained that dreams are not just mere chance but something which has been pre-arranged by some supernatural powers or by a guardian angel. Jung maintained that "Dreams are the facts from which we must proceed."[1] Equally, the kind of dreams which arouse great interest are those which predict the future, or coincide with the event. People tend to ask "how did you know?" In my case I tell them I did not know but the dream told me.

Dreaming of Going to York on 29th October, 1994

I did not tell my niece about the journey I intended to make and never mentioned I was going to take her. I kept quiet. As the week approached, I thought it was right to mention it. I told her I was going to a writers' conference in Yorkshire and she could come if she wanted. Upon hearing the name 'York' she said, "The lady who teaches me English told me about the dream she had last week." She dreamed she was showing my niece where York is on the map. The lady actually took her to York showing her different places. I found this very fascinating and failed to understand. Why should she dream about York of all cities, when we were going there that week?

However, I interpreted the dream to my niece although I felt the dream was straightforward. The tutor was showing her all the places of interest and actually took her there. It follows then that I myself took the role of her tutor. It could be that some people dream the opposite. It could be one person doing something in the dream, whereas in reality another person does it. However, it is not the characters who are of primary importance to me, but rather the outcome of the dream.

Interestingly, the seminar was not in York. When the letter had come to notify me of the seminar, I had read the word Yorkshire, and had taken it for granted that it was in York. I have never been to York and, I being excited to hear the word Yorkshire, concluded it was taking place in York. It was in my mind because I had been wanting to see York. Upon reaching York, I started checking on the map to see where Skipton was. I couldn't find it on the map. I thought of asking at the Tourist Information Centre, and was told the place is in Leeds. That is why I could not find it on the map. I was supposed to take another train going to Leeds and there take yet another. We would not make it for the seminar. I said: "We might as well spend a day in York, because I have never been there. So we had to go to York, perhaps to fulfil the dream. Every time I go anywhere, I always check the map before leaving Liverpool, but this time I failed to do so. To this extent one could say that a dream is precognition. It tells you what you are going to do. It foresees the future.

Dreams in the Bible

As with the prophets in the Bible, it was believed that the faculty was provided by the gods or spirits. For example, "Pharaoh's dream of seven lean kine eating the seven fat kine, and the seven thin ears of corn eating the seven fat ears"[2] was provided by God. Joseph interpreted it, and the interpretation became true. Dreams in the Bible also come to warn against evil. Evil as well as good seems to follow the continuity of history, and every generation produces its crafty tyrants who misuse their power. But the wise men who came to Bethlehem were fortunately forewarned against the subtle flattery of the king. Their bad dreams about Herod's true intention enabled them to outwit his wickedness. In biblical times people often thought of bad dreams as warnings from God. Parker, in *Healing Dreams*, agrees with the idea of God providing dreams. "Dreams are a gift from a loving God and they are intended for our good."[3] Job was of the opinion that dreams come to us when we have hardened our hearts not to listen to God's word. "For God speaks in one way and two, though man does not perceive it. In a dream, in a vision of the night, when deep sleep falls upon men, while they slumber on their beds, then he opens the ears of men, and terrifies them with warnings, that he may turn man aside from his deed."[4]

Talking in a Dream

My niece dreamed of a wonderful wedding. She talks when she is dreaming as though she were in trance. So my sister listened to what she was saying. "This is a wonderful wedding," she said. My sister said to her "That is not a wedding you are seeing in your dream, it is a funeral." My sister was explaining to her again in the morning, just emphasising that it was a funeral not a wedding of which she was dreaming.

Not long after they saw someone coming in a car saying there was a telephone call which came from Zimbabwe, and that my other sister had died. My sister said to my niece, "Do you see now what I was telling you?" Actually the man who brought the message found them at the same spot where they were discussing the dream. As we see in this dream at home in Malawi, and apparently the whole of Africa, some dream and some are busy interpreting dreams. My sister was more willing to accept her daughter's dream and interpret it. To this extent it could be said that it is our African belief that a dream is not to be dismissed as just implausible. It carries the connotation of probability.

I related my dream with that of McNish as recorded by Inglis. He dreamt of the death of a near relation. "Waking up in 'inconceivable terror' [McNish's own description] he had immediately written to the man's family. His letter had crossed with one from them telling him that the relation, though he appeared to have been in perfect health, had died – on the morning of the dream."[5]

By the same token, although some regard dreams as irrational, in my view they should be taken as a guide to tell us about the present and the future. Inglis stated: "But the essential point is that the way our dreams present themselves, infantile though they often are, should not be allowed to delude us into dismissing them as unworthy of our attention."[6]

Rosalind Cartwright in *Night Life* stated that "Dreaming has effects on waking attention."[7] My niece's dream reflected upon my sister's death. Cartwright goes on to say, "When a dream has taken place, we awake ready to shift attention to active engagement with reality. When it has not, our focus of attention drifts back to subjective inner material."[8] A dream also helps us to cope with situations, as Cartwright also observed. "Dreams appear to regulate the subjective world of feelings and help us adapt to stressful experiences so that we can handle them more realistically during waking."[9]

However, whilst my niece was dreaming of a wonderful wedding, she was in reality dreaming about my sister's death. Here we can see that dream interpretation is useful. You dream of something whilst in actual fact you are dreaming the opposite. Moore supports this theory propounded by the African society. Thus, she states: "To dream of a wedding portends a funeral near you."[10]

The same dream could be treated as a prophetic dream and to some extent a psychic or precognitive dream. In this we see how powerful the mind is in its ability to reach out to the future.

Moore comments on the same thing when she says, "There have been many strange instances of individual prophetic dreams and these are, by and large, very definite instances of the power of the mind to reach out the future."[11] She adds: "Accept also that your mind can reach out into the immediate future and foretell what might happen."[12] As in the case of my niece's dream, it was only four hours after her dream that my sister died. The dream was referring to the immediate future.

My niece's dream could also be seen by some people as a coincidence. My sister was interpreting the dream to her in the morning and before she finished someone came with a message. Actually my sister died the very morning of the dream.

I was frustrated and depressed when my sister died in February. Since she was not sick, her death shocked me and I couldn't stop crying. I could not travel immediately because my passport had expired. I then went to London to sort out my passport. I stayed with a family from home. The night before, the husband said he was going to work first, and go to town after to arrange about my travel. I then told the wife I was going to stay late in bed. Whilst sleeping I had a dream at 8.45. The wife stood by the door facing their car; I myself stood on the other side of the car. It was as if the car was between us. My eyes looked for the other end of the car. I saw my mother, who died in May, 1993, coming towards me. I jumped and ran hastily to meet her. I grabbed her and she sat down. I slept on her knees. Both of us started crying together. When we had finished crying, my mother vanished. I never saw her either then or thereafter. That was the end of the dream. I myself woke up. I get up each time I finish dreaming. From this I deduced that those who die can still arrive and see us. So she came to help me cry and let me know that she was well aware.

Honestly, after this dream I never cried again until I reached Zimbabwe. I interpreted the dream to mean that my mother was saying, "I am with you in this sorrow." I was indeed comforted after seeing my mother in the dream. The dream also came as an encouragement. I strongly believe both my mother, my father and my two sisters who died are truly alive somewhere. My sister, who died in 1995, was very happy the day before she died. It was as if she knew she was dying.

Fire at the Queen's House at Windsor

I normally dream in the morning. The time was 7.00 a.m. when I had this dream. I saw the Queen's house in flames of fire. The Queen was walking round through all the rooms while the house was burning. She had put on a royal long dress and her crown. She was walking through all those rooms steadily and was not frightened of the fire. The dress was just as it is in the pictures, with no indication of being burned. But her face changed. It went dark like charcoal. Throughout that dream the Queen spent time going round all the rooms, and the rooms were empty. The dream ended whilst the Queen was still going round.

Honestly, I thought this was a silly dream. I said to myself: "What on earth is the Queen doing, walking in fire and her clothes are not burned?" So I dismissed the dream as madness. I did not bother to write it down. I normally share dreams with colleagues when I go to work, but since I thought such a thing could not happen, I kept quiet, but even so I was puzzled. I came back from work and put on the six o'clock news and the first item I heard was about the Queen's house, Windsor Castle, going on fire. I told one of my friends, Grace Jal-wang, the following day, after the incident had already happened. Grace said, "But Mary, why did you not say so?" There was no opportunity to tell anyone. The incident happened the very same day and I was very busy at work.

Another colleague, who is a very devoted Christian, argued that the dreams I had described in the first book could have been prevented. She thinks I could have prayed and God would have changed the situation. My knowledge is limited on this; probably the theologians would have the right answer. Grace Jal-wang was referring to the same thing, thinking the fire could have been prevented. But then, yet again, who am I to have authority to tell things concerning the Royal family? Yet again the problem with a dream is that it tells you what is going to happen, but it does not tell you the exact date and time. Equally, who would have listened to me? They would have dismissed it as illogical.

If I had been at home in Malawi, and had had a dream that the President's house was going to be on fire, people would have taken it seriously, and they would have tried to prevent it by being on the alert. But then there are elderly people there who would have been very much concerned to interpret it. A lot of them would have interpreted it to mean war. But my dreams are straightforward. If it says 'fire' then fire there must be, not something else. Whatever I dream comes in the same manner. However, a dream, although some people might regard it as a coincidence, does give an insight. This is in agreement with what Soozi Holbeche wrote, "To ask a dream for insight, information or healing, to use dreams to solve problems, is as valid for us today as it was for the ancient Greeks and Egyptians." [13]

Dreaming While in a Lift

But first another dream, which a colleague at work, Julie McColl, felt was silly and dismissed. Thus she writes in her own words, "Last night/morning I dreamt about my friend, Carol Brady, who is off sick from work at the moment and has been for a number of weeks. I remember in the dream being surprised at seeing her in our lift at work and asking her how long she had been back. The evening before I had started to browse through your book, picking out a few dreams, and was wondering what I would dream about myself On awakening I dismissed my dream about my friend and thought I must telephone her sometime."

"I met another colleague for lunch today and asked if she had spoken to Carol and to ask how she was. My friend informed me that she had spoken to her and that she was returning to work tomorrow, 15.4.93. I was stunned and explained to my friend that I had dreamt about her in our work's lift. I can't wait for tonight's episode."

Pharaoh's Boat

There are also some dreams which hold strong conviction for the dreamer, but become difficult to convince the public about. Soozi gives a very interesting account of this. It is the story of Ahmed Youssef Moustafa, of Egypt. His dreams were meaningful and practical. They provided an inspiration for his life and work. He acted on dream incubation (waiting for the dream to come), and had recurring dreams of ancient Egypt while sleeping in the pyramids. He saw in his dreams how the pigments were mixed for painting pictures, statues and mummies. He saw how the hieroglyphic characters were applied to the walls and understood their meaning.

When he was nineteen years of age, he heard that the Cairo Museum was looking for someone to rebuild or restore the skeleton of a boat buried near the Cheops Pyramid. He was excited and sent his application. But this was turned down because he had no formal qualifications. He told them he knew how to do it through his dreams, but became a laughing stock when they heard that his knowledge was derived from dreams. The job was re-advertised but in vain, as no one knew how to restore that boat. Later on the authorities had no choice and sent for him. He started the work and finished it. As Soozi Holbeche puts it, "This boat, supposed to be the one that carried the pharaoh to the under world, is now completely restored and can be seen displayed alongside the Pyramid of Cheops." [14]

Dream Precognition

Here is yet another precognitive dream. A colleague at work, Nargis Anwar, had shared with me her husband's dreams. The husband wrote in his own words, "I was back at home in 1992 amongst my family. My mother came up to me and said 'Look after yourself; make sure you don't fall, for if you break anything (meaning – breaking any bone of my body), it will be difficult at your age to get it fixed again.' She repeated, 'Just watch yourself'.

"I woke up – this was in the afternoon – I used to sleep after lunch time and I worked in the evenings. I had a catering business. I went to the take-away. After being there for only half an hour, I slipped very badly. I was so lucky that I didn't break any bone of my body. I then remembered my dream and my mother's words. She has been dead for 24 years."

The dream above was premonition. It was both a warning and guiding dream. It is as I have put it in my first book, *The Usefulness of Dreams*, that our ancestors still influence our African culture. Mr. Anwar, who had this dream, is from Pakistan; as such, it could be said that this is also true of some people in Pakistan. The incident happened the same day Mr. Anwar had the dream.

Another premonition is recorded of Charles Dickens, from an account in his biography. As Rhine puts it, "[Dickens] dreamed of a visitor whom he would meet at tea the next day, heard her introduced, heard her name, which was strange to him. The next day he met the lady just as dreamed." [15]

Not a Dream but Words

Sometimes one does not really have to dream. One says something and it happens. But as usual we don't take note of what someone is saying, more importantly if it is a child. A lady, Mrs. Joan Sanders of Knowsley village, reported on the sudden death of her son, David Sanders, who died on 6th August, 1970, in a road accident. David was 12 years old. "I played silly games with the children, David and his friend, Billy, in my living room using a Ouija Board. David, spinning the pointer, suddenly announced that Frank, the person from the other place, spoke to him. I asked what Frank had said; he replied that the message had been for him and Billy. Later that same evening David said to me, 'Mum, when I die don't let them put me down a hole will you?' I felt cold as ice and said 'That's not for me to say; you make those arrangements with your children when they grow up.' But he said again quite calm, 'I am asking that you don't let them put me down a hole in the dark.'"

"I learned after the accident that David had gone for the day to the beach with a school friend, Alan, and one parent. When they arrived, after a walk, a few games and the picnic, the boys decided to build a cross in the sand. Underneath the cross he wrote 'David Sanders, 6th August, 1970.' It was pointed out to him that he had made a mistake that that day was the fourth. He replied that the date was right and refused to change it. He died on 6th August, 1970.

"That morning he went out with a different boy and refused to change into fresh clothes. He had left off his watch, took no money apart from his bus fare, hugged me – nearly choked me would be a better description – danced out, turned and waved, and that was the last time I saw him.

"I have dreamt of him once since he died and seen him clearly not as a 12 year-old boy but as a young man grown amazingly like my eldest son Allan. Maybe that's because his brother was his hero."

It seems to me that there is truly a continuity of life in the other world. The dream above seems to indicate just that: the experience of dreaming of someone who died years ago and seeing him as a grown-up person. I had a dream just after my mother had died in May, 1993. I saw her just as she was in February, 1993. She was even putting on her normal, ordinary clothes. When I dreamt about my father, who died thirty years ago, I saw him as very old in the dream. He looked really old, and was using a stick to walk. This too gave me the impression that he was alive and continues to live.

As I stated above, sometimes you don't have to dream, your unconscious reveals what is hidden. Rhine gives an account of a girl who lived in Ohio (USA). She went to visit her aunt in Florida. While she was washing dishes, she thought she heard her father calling her name, 'Betty Lou'. In her own words, "I ran to the door and opened it, fully expecting to see my dad, but nobody was there." [16] The girl related the story to her aunt. Her aunt advised her to ring home in case her dad wanted to talk to her. She did as advised. She rang and her mother answered the phone.

160

"Oh honey, it's you; Daddy's calling for you. The doctor's here now. Daddy had a heart attack." [17]

On Monday, 5.12.94., I was bored with reading and decided to go to Tesco's shop to buy milk etc. On my way back I decided to ring a colleague in London. I rang just to get his comments on the talk I had given. I rang on my way to my house, thinking of catching him before he went out after lunch. It was 12.15 p.m. when I rang his house and nobody picked up the phone. I came back and thought of checking the post again, although I knew I had already checked before going to Tesco's. That was 12.30 p.m. and, to my amazement, I found a letter from my friend whom I was ringing containing the information I had required. It is strange because he does not normally write.

It is always the case with me that when I am thinking of someone, either a letter or a telephone call is on its way. Another interesting thing: I cleared my flat on 19th December, throwing away the chairs I had. This is because my friends from Runcorn, Mr. and Mrs. E.B. Kewley, were giving me their three-piece suite. I had a visitor that same day. The visitor had been to my place once. Apparently she was just wondering in her heart as to where the chairs had gone, but did not want to ask since she was not yet used to me. Later she thought of asking me. "Where are the chairs?" I said I had thrown them away and that my friends were bringing some new chairs. She commented: "I think they are now on their way; that's why I have asked." Within a minute the door bell rang and it was truly the Kewleys bringing the chairs.

Dreaming of Dead Animals

Some dreams may appear complicated, though. One of the Service Managers, Chris Clarke, had just been on a holiday with her husband. Whilst there she had a dream which puzzled her. She saw dead animals in very clear water. The animals all resembled African animals such as lions, hyenas, leopards, etc.

Upon hearing the dream, I immediately interpreted it to mean

161

'full of life' or 'abundance of life' if you like. Yet again, anything to do with clear water also symbolises righteousness.

On hearing my interpretation, she quickly asked: "What about these dead animals; what do they actually mean?" Anything dead at home also means long life. If you dream someone died it means he/she is going to live a long life. So these dead animals might also be associated with life. Moore, in her book *Dream Book*, also stated: "Death – This is a dream of contradictions; it augurs happy long life. To the single it denotes an honourable and happy marriage." In the tarot cards "Death means a new start".[18]

Chris went on to say most of her dreams solve the day-to-day problems of life. In this sense a dream could be seen as a problem solver.

Conclusion

I would like to conclude this chapter by quoting Cartwright again when he asserted: "The psychotherapist knows that uncovering dream meanings can have very real effects on a patient's waking life." Dreams relate to real life situations, as we have seen in that my niece's dream concerned my sister's death. And it is more powerful to predict the immediate future. It can also act as a coincidence. It is as if the one dying sends a message to the dreamer.

Bibliography

1. Jung, C.G., *Memories, Dreams, Reflections*, p. 194, by Collins, London & Glasgow 1961.
2. Inglis, B., *Coincidence: A Matter of Chance – Or Synchronicity*, p. 66, Hutchinson, London, Sydney, Auckland & Johannesburg, 1990.
3. Parker, R., *Healing Dreams*, p. 8, SPCK, London, 1988.
4. Job 33, vs. 14-17, RSV.
5. Inglis, B., *The Power of Dreams*, p. 98, Grafton Books, Great Britain, 1988.

6. Ibid. p. 204.

7. Cartwright R., *Night Life*, p. 131, Prentice-Hall, Inc., U.S.A., 1977.

8. Ibid. p. 131.

9. Ibid. p. 131.

10. Moore, O., *Dream Book*, p. 95, W. Foulsham & Co. Ltd., London, Toronto, New York, Cape Town & Sydney, 1985

11. Ibid. p. 9.

12. Ibid. p. 9.

13. Holbeche, S., *The Power of Dreams*, p. 111, Piatkus, Great Britain, 1991.

14. Ibid. p. 112.

15. Rhine, L., *Hidden Channels of The Mind*, p. 29, Victor Gollanez Ltd., London, 1962.

16. Ibid. p. 134.

17. Ibid. p. 134.

18. Moores. O., op. cit. p. 63.

Conclusion

As I now see it, I could conclude this book by saying that parapsychology is nothing but the study of psychology itself, since it deals with certain anomalous experiences and behaviour. It also overlaps with the physical, biological and social sciences, as well as mathematics, for its methodology; and with philosophy for both its methods and its theory. Professor R. Morris agrees that "Parapsychology may acquire a sufficiently solid data base and associated cohesive theory to be regarded as a separate discipline, but that time is not yet."

There are however, some problems attached to parapsychology. For example some sceptics, like the psychologist C.E.M. Hansel, have asserted that "psi is not possible because it contradicts the laws of physics." Eysenck et al. agree to the above assertion and state that "We are psychologists, but we do not feel qualified to make such categorical assertions about physics. The most important thing is to examine their logic (do they make some kind of sense?) and consider whether they are scientific models (do they make testable predictions?)."

Robert Morris also points out that "Others suspect that some extensive modification of present-day physics will be called for, but that it will probably still be called physics when the day is done. And still others, such as myself, feel that we are not yet sure enough of our facts to have strong views about the likely nature of psychic events, save for acceptance of the fact that much of what is labelled psychic turns out to have fairly ordinary explanations and some clever deceptions."

Most of the experiments done in parapsychology do not produce confirmation or refutation of the concept of psi. Susan

Blackmoore also supports this when she asks "What do these negative results tell us? of course the one thing they do not tell us is that psi does not exist." Susan Blackmoore then concludes that "Where there is no rational and convincing answer, belief takes over, and that is why there are two sides, and such misunderstanding."

Gertrude Schmeidler also supports Blackmoore. Like Blackmoore, she starts with a question. If the perception or prediction is justified, could it be said the hypothesis has been proved? Some intellectuals, however, believe that to reason like this or to take this as a proof should be regarded as a fallacy. This argument is based on scientific method, which asserts that if 'A' is true then 'B' must also be true. In a similar manner, if the hypothesis is true then the perception will also be true. This could go on and on. 'A' always starts, but if it is vice-versa that 'B' is true, 'A' may in this circumstance be false. This theory holds, as Gertrude Schmeidler puts it: "Logicians tell us that verifying a prediction is never proof of a hypothesis." It follows, then, that the scientific method can disprove but not prove. But since parapsychology is an area of investigation, it remains true to say that one cannot affirm but can only say the evidence supports the hypothesis. With this difficulty most parapsychologists tend to pass a personal value judgement, as Blackmoore has already pointed out above. Perhaps I could add that if one is positive, psi phenomena tend to happen very often, whereas they do not happen to those with a negative attitude.

For the arguments stated above one could say that parapsychology will continue to be controversial for some time. People who have experienced it will not be quiet. Since it involves the study of human observation and interpretation of events, it will one day be the very best of scientific study. Parapsychology has been associated with socially problematic situations. It has been regarded as threatening to major established beliefs, both theistic and secular, of how the world works. It has been linked to pathological problems. The field has been ignored by scientists. When we ignore something, as Professor Morris pointed out, "We promote ignorance." Most people want a better understanding of psychic experiences since it affects a lot of people in society.

Although some people have doubts on psi, it is equally true to say many people have experience of psi. For this reason I would like to conclude the book by pointing out that people's abilities differ. From my experience, however, I have attributed psychic, synchronicity, seriality and dream as things revealed by God. Both Geulinex and Leibnitz, as I have pointed out in chapter 5, also regarded the co-ordination of the psychic and the physical as an act of God, of some principle standing outside empirical nature.

In some parts of the book I have related ESP to brain, but Jung himself was of the contention that we must completely give up the idea of the psyche's being somehow connected with the brain, and remember instead the 'meaningful' or 'intelligent' behaviour of the lower organisms, which are without a brain. They are to some extent independent in themselves. They are a progression of God's creation. They slowly reveal God's nature to us.